Escape Room Time
Activity Time

ESCAPE THE HIGH SEAS

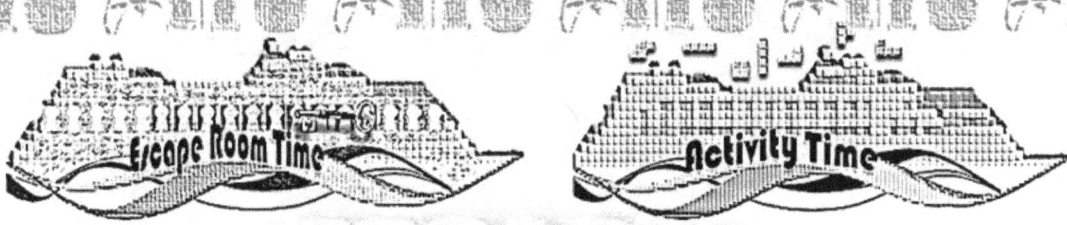

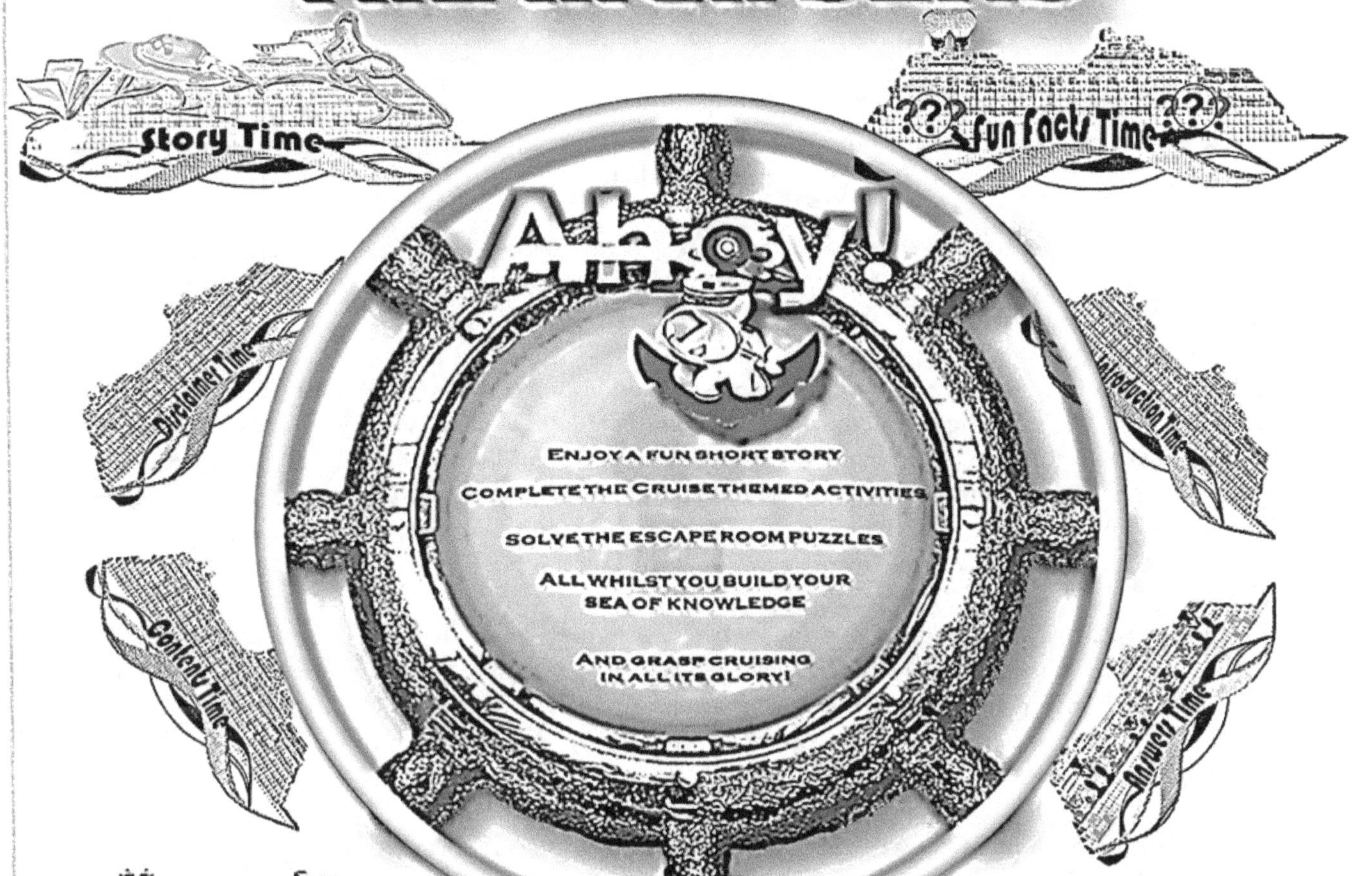

Story Time
Fun Facts Time
Ahoy!
ENJOY A FUN SHORT STORY
COMPLETE THE CRUISE THEMED ACTIVITIES
SOLVE THE ESCAPE ROOM PUZZLES
ALL WHILST YOU BUILD YOUR SEA OF KNOWLEDGE
AND GRASP CRUISING IN ALL ITS GLORY!
Disclaimer Time
Introduction Time
Contents Time
Answers Time
Colouring Time
Ship Time

CRUISING THROUGH ONE ACTIVITY AT A TIME

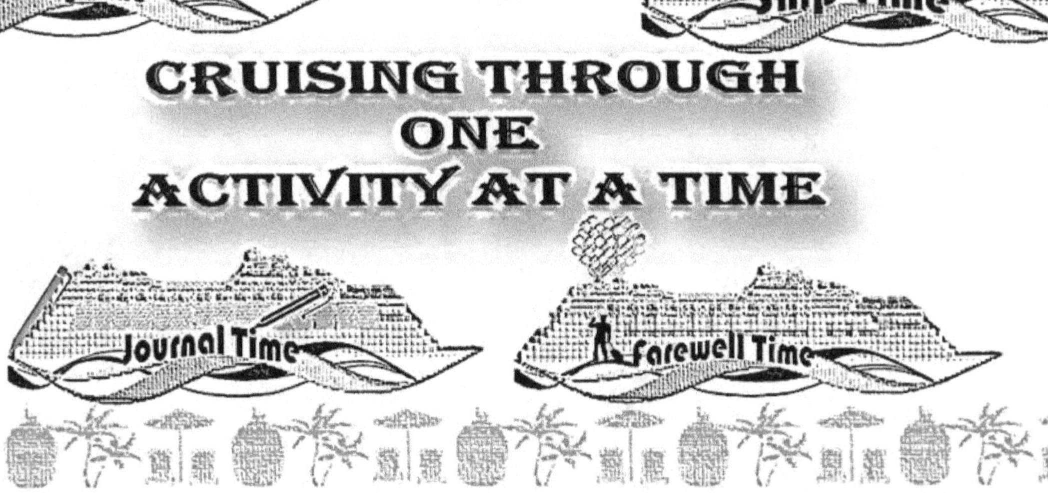

Journal Time
Farewell Time

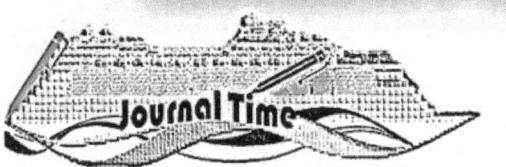

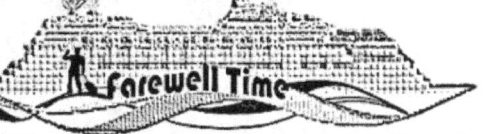

Disclaimer Time

Copyright © 2024 by G E Riding
All rights reserved.

No portion of this book may be reproduced in any form without written permission from the publisher, illustrator, or author, except as permitted by Australian copyright law.

No part of this publication may be reproduced, distributed, or transmitted in any form or by any means, including photocopying, recording, or other electronic or mechanical methods, without the prior written permission of the publisher, illustrator, or author, except as permitted by Australian copyright law.

The content of this book is for informational purposes only and is not intended to be advice or to be relied upon without consulting your travel agent or cruise company. The content is limited, basic, and is not a complete guide. You understand that this book is of the author's experiences and opinions and is for entertainment. It is not intended as a substitute for consultation with a licensed travel provider or expert. The information may be correct at the time of publishing but may have changed after that date. Please consult with your own travel specialist regarding the suggestions, opinions and recommendations made in this book.

Although the publisher, illustrator and the author have made every effort to ensure the contents are specific experiences of the author; the publisher, illustrator and the author assume no responsibility for errors, inaccuracies, omissions, or any other inconsistencies herein and hereby disclaim any liability to any party for any loss, damage, or disruption caused by errors or omissions, whether such errors or omissions result from negligence, accident, or any other cause.

The content of this book may have some puzzles or words beyond the capability of the age of a young user, and we recommend friends and or family participation, to enhance their experience.

The use of this book implies your acceptance of this disclaimer.

Book Cover by G E Riding
Illustrations by G E Riding
Author G E Riding & Ceejay Riding
ISBN Paperback colour edition 978-1-7635077-4-6
ISBN Paperback Black & White edition 978-1-7635077-3-9

Contents

Content	Page#	Content	Page#
Colouring- Story Time-An a'moo'sing pack	6 & 7	Slides & ladders activity	51
Escape Room - Puzzle #1	**8 & 9**	Fun facts – environmental facts	52
Fun facts - packing hints	10	Which pipe fills up first? activity	53
Colouring page - packing tips	11	Find the Differences – **washy washy**	54
Unscramble words - around the globe	12	**Story Time– Balancing the Difference**	**55**
Colouring page - cruise fun facts	13	**Escape Room Puzzle - #6**	**56 & 57**
Draw a cruise - ship bon voyage	14	Fun facts – Balancing food & Ship	58
Story Time-Tuned to Cruising	**15**	Fill in a word – balancing facts	59
Escape Room - Puzzle #2	**16 & 17**	Fun facts – cruise ships	60
Rebus puzzle - cruise companies	18	Connect the facts – ship locations	61
Colouring page - travellers	19	Fun facts – knots & ship navigation	62
Code breaker - cruise fun facts	20 & 21	Navigation maze & distance puzzle	63
Fun facts ship - rank hierarchy fun facts	22	Find a word – ship features	64
Story Time- Farm to the Palms	**23**	**Story Time- Cruising One Port at a Time**	**65**
Escape Room - Puzzle # 3	**24 & 25**	**Escape Room Puzzle - # 7**	**66 & 67**
Colouring page/drawing ship & carving	26	Connect the letters – ship power	68
Find the pictures - I spy farm to ship	27	Colouring page – port hole & sea life	69
Jokes fun cruise humour	28	Learn to draw – crab & octopus	70
Trivia - cruise themed	29	Crossword – sun safety	71
Maze – road trip navigation	30	Fun facts – cruise ships in port	72
Crossword – road trip co-ordinates	31	Colouring page – turtle & fun facts	73
Find a word – road safety	32	Maze – port to ship	74
Fill a word – road safety fun puzzler	33	Colouring page – port picture	75
Colouring page – anchor of cruising	34	Colouring page – doodle art	76
Story Time– Welcome Aboard	**35**	**Story Time- Sea Days & Ways to Play**	**77**
Escape Room - Puzzle - # 4	**36 & 37**	**Escape Room Puzzle # 8**	**78 & 79**
Fill in card – travel ticket	38	Sudoku – billiards table & facts	80
Draw & colour – passport activity	39	Who did it puzzle – mutiny on the ship	81
Colouring page – welcome aboard	40	Fun facts & Colouring page – ocean life	82
Colour code grid – balloon drop	41	Find the hidden items – deep ocean	83
Find a word – muster drill	42	Colouring page – art of the seas	84
Fill in a word – muster station	43	**Story Time-Fun Adventures on the Hunt**	**85**
Find the deck – onboard activity	44	**Escape Room Puzzle - # 9**	**86 & 87**
Story Time-Seas the Cruising Way	**45**	Fun facts – sailor & ship superstitions	88
Escape Room - Puzzle #5	**46 & 47**	Scavenger hunt – onboard activity	89
Fun facts – making a towel animal	48	Who am I? activity	90
Track the ball – putt putt (mini) golf	49	Who am I? activity - riddles	91
Slides & ladders – sign language	50	Find the ducks	92

Contents

Content	Page #
Story Time – Some 'Sea'rious Vacay'ing	93
Escape Room Puzzle - #10	**94 & 95**
Fun facts – ships flags	96
Colour your own flag – signal your name	97
Fun facts – ship's horn	98
Maze – Marco Polo	99
Find a word – phonetic alphabet	100
Story Time – Waving Goodbye The end	**101**
Don't risk it for the biscuit! Disembarking	102
Escape Room Codes in the safe	**103**
Escape room – note from the safe	104
Escape room – certificate of accomplishment	105
Glossary of Terms	106 - 111
Free space for a photo or drawing	112, 114, 132, 140
Your cruise travel journal	**113 - 140**
Answer sheets	141 - 153

Content	Page #
Your daily planner	115 - 118
Your journal time	119 – 132
Your port/island time	133 – 136
Your new friends	137 - 140

Introduction

This book is full of thrilling cruise activities that will ignite your thirst for adventure. Whether you're completing this alone or with family and friends, it's designed for solo, friendly competition, and bonding.

The puzzles vary in difficulty, offering challenges suitable for all ages and skill levels within a family. Created to unite individuals, evoke happiness and tears of joy, providing entertainment that immerses you in a realm of discovery, empowering you to embrace cruising.

Seas the day & Sail away

Before and during your cruise, you'll face challenges feeling like a real apprentice crew member navigating the high seas.

Hidden ducks may appear with every page, an escape room puzzle awaits, and the plank walk is a test of survival.

Besides puzzles and activities, this book will teach you about cruising through quirky, fun facts, turning you into a master cruiser.

Also, join Cindy on a journey through her exciting holiday, from the farm to the island palms, in a journal packed with fun facts and activities about cruising.

It is a perfect Vitamin Sea for cruising!

The storyline

The story is about a country teen, Cindy, who explores cruising for the first time, experiencing sights she has never seen.

From her usual life on the farm, Cindy ventures to the island palms, the creek to the seas, and cruising to islands she has never been. On her pathway to having fun, she records her trip in a journal from day one.

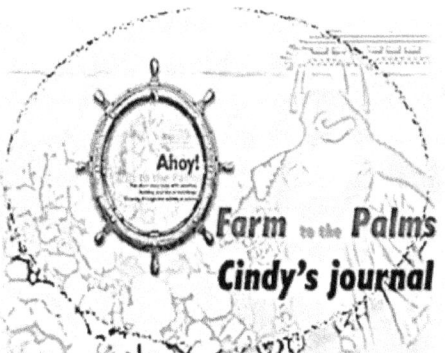

Be careful, before you enter Cindy's journal, you will enter an escape room. Even after escaping all the rooms, don't forget to decode the secret message, otherwise you may meet your doom.

Discover a new world of cruising through Cindy's life by completing activities, puzzles, and reading fun facts. You may find yourself laughing at some old wise cracks.

Let your cleverness cruise through Cindy's exciting adventure story and challenge yourself with the puzzles and take the glory.

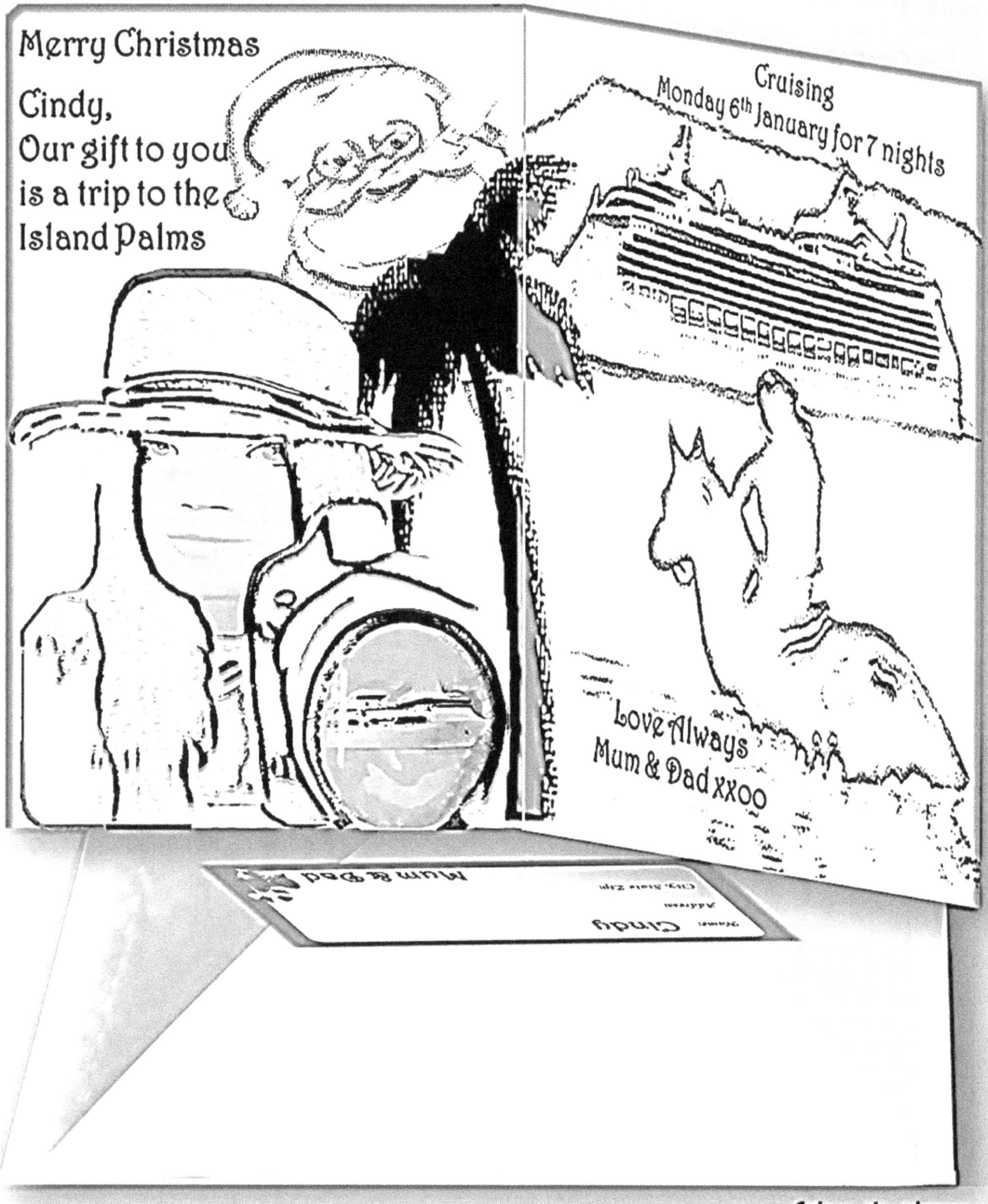

Merry Christmas

Cindy,
Our gift to you
is a trip to the
Island Palms

Cruising
Monday 6th January for 7 nights

Love Always
Mum & Dad xxoo

Colour the picture

An a"moo"sing pack — Cindy's Journal Entry One

Dear Journal,

Loved the Christmas card from Mom and Dad—a holiday cruise to the Island Palms!—has me overjoyed and ready for a break from school and my chores on our farm.

Today it was time to pack, so I took my bag out the back. Even though it looked very odd, mom just smiled and gave me a nod.

The bag was full of dust, so it made sense to clean it outside without a fuss.

After setting the bag down, I glanced back at the kitchen window and saw Mom laughing like a clown. Thinking I was in trouble, I sighed, only to realize Mom wasn't sad; it was something funny in my bag.

I looked down and there was my favourite calf named Daisy lying on my gear. Mom, still laughing, yelled out, 'We don't think she will pass through customs; nice try Cindy dear, now bring that bag in here.'

I had made Daisy a comfy straw bed so she could relax in the barn, distracting her from my holiday ahead.

I kissed Daisy, promised to see her soon, and told her not to worry as I had to take the bag back to my room. I grabbed my bag and headed back inside. Walking past mom, she playfully took it all in her stride.

I assured mum I would pack more clothes, my headphones, and some summer shoes. Mom gave me a list of some hints, and I was happy, as it had a lot of valuable clues.

In my room, I chose my Crocs rather than my cotton-farm work shoes that I wear around the crops.

I then grabbed my clothes, put them onto the bed in a pile, and I tried them on to see what was an appropriate beach style. I realised that on the farm, my country clothing is more suited for the cattle droving. I realise we are going on a summer vacay, and I can't wait to be cruising on our way.

Cruising Life; Thanks for today, can't wait for my holiday!

Story continues Page 15 Colour the picture

7

ESCAPE ROOM #1
Enter if you dare

Unlock Cindy's journal

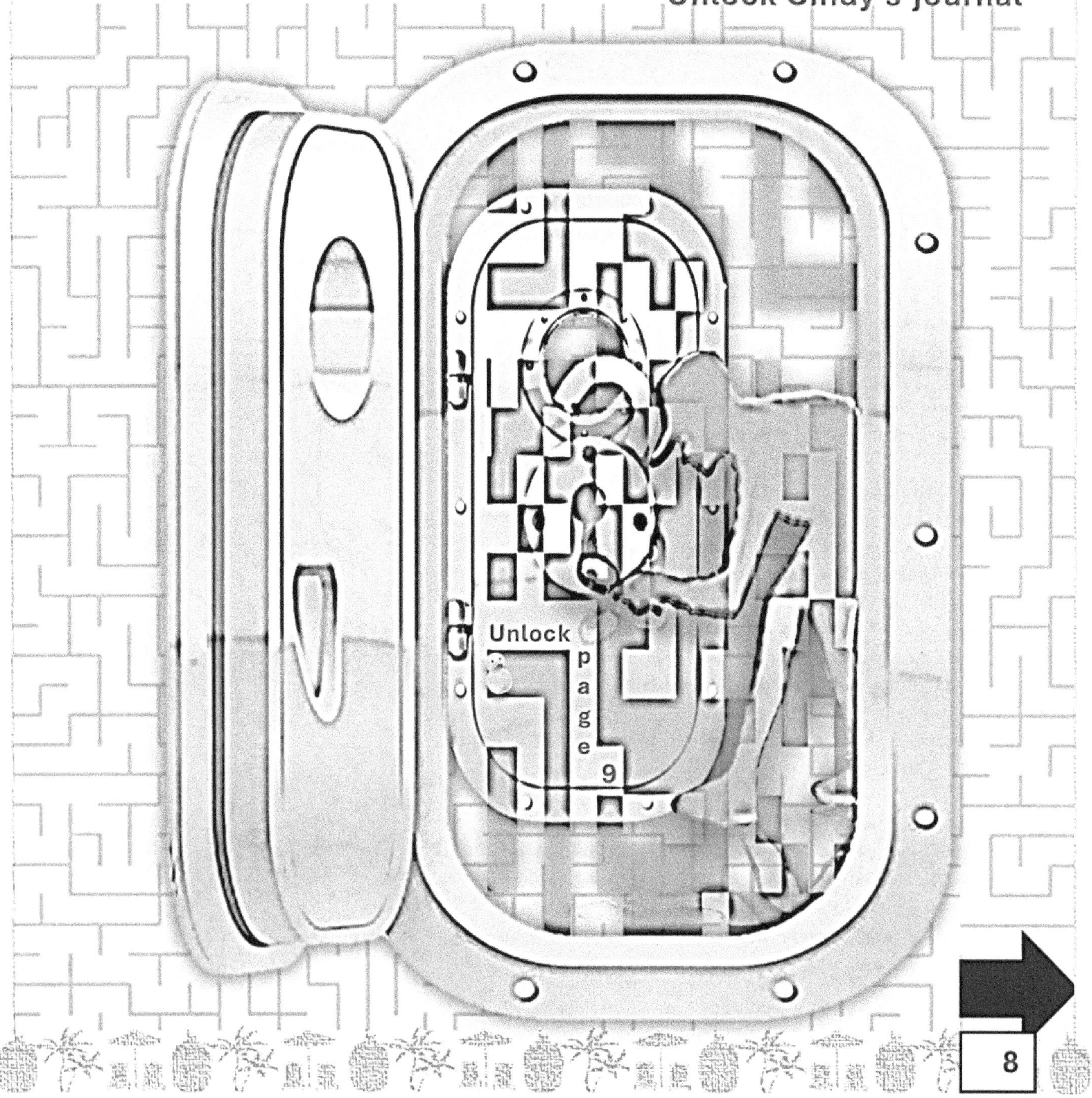

Unlock page 9

8

Escape, but don't make a mistake!

Oh no Cindy's journal is locked. You must solve puzzles to get out and through each section of her adventures before the ship docks.

1	2	1	2	1	2
3	4	3	1	4	1
1	4	1	3	4	3
2	4	4	4	4	4
1	3	1	3	4	3
2	3	1	1	4	1
1	2	3	2	1	2

1 = Light Blue

2 = Dark Blue

3 = Black

4 = Red

Colour the numbers to reveal the number code that unlocks Cindy's journal and the pathway to her activities. Write the code (number) in the box below.

Also, write the code on page 103

Answers on page 142

Some hints on what to pack to keep you on track!

Cindy packed by looking at this list, see if there is anything you have missed.

Tick when you have checked each item category

Suncream / After sun cream ☐	t-shirts ☐	Shorts/skirts or dresses Don't forget your long pants, for when it cools down ☐	bathing suits/swimwear ☐
Nice casual dinner clothes ☐	long sleeve shirts or sweatshirt/jumper/wind jacket, for colder days ☐	Toothbrush Toothpaste Special soaps Shampoo & Conditioner ☐	Formal wear, if you are going to formal nights ☐
Underwear/garments Socks ☐	Camera Binoculars ☐	For a Baby Diapers, bibs, bottles, formula, baby food, dummy, rash cream, teething gel, swim diapers, medication ☐	Sleepwear/pyjamas ☐
Belts/ties and something to put your sea pass in (Lanyard) ☐	Hairbrush, Hair accessories ☐	Hats and sunglasses ☐	Activity pack, pencils, books and small toys ☐
Shoes, joggers, sandals, beach shoes, dress shoes ☐	Beach toys, beach bag, swim safe and goggles, snorkel set ☐	Carry-on bag for medications, documents extra clothes, until your staterooms are available (not too heavy) ☐	Sea sickness tablets or medications for example Panadol/aspirin ☐

We suggest for you to pack colored pencils, and some string to make some knots.

**Legal Documents
Passports
Cruise documents
Driver's licence/ ID
DON'T PLACE IN SUITCASE** ☐

We recommend that you enjoy your cruise and have some fun, by smiling lots.

Colouring Time

Get ready for your cruise trip, here is another packing tip!

Don't forget to take your camera.

There will be a lot of memories to remember.

You are in for a fun and fabulous treat! There are lots of activities on board to keep you on your feet! Colour the picture or draw a picture of you playing on the cruise ship.

Full throttle forward in cruise mode Where the adventure happens all around the globe

Unscramble the words that represent activities that you may experience on board a cruise ship

vmioes _____

ekictingsa _____

rseadsitlwe _____

kbeabtasll _____

mwigmnis _____

flgioimn _____

deaarc _____

qaarkpua _____

duskcbil _____

rerctaroelsol _____

rnmkilocbcig _____

ezinipl _____

Colour the picture

Answers on page 142

Draw a picture on the Hull

Colour the ship, for your wonderful trip.

Cruising Fun facts...  **The RADOMES may signal your phones!**

The large white balls on top of cruise ships are called Radomes. The name is split into two parts; the Radar and Dome. The dome covers important equipment such as; the radar, satellite and navigational hardware, protecting them from the weather. They are important for you and all the guests as the balls also provide you with internet access whilst on board. Their position is essential for the ship's communications and the balls protects it all from the weather elements.

Bon Voyage!
French, for; "good journey"

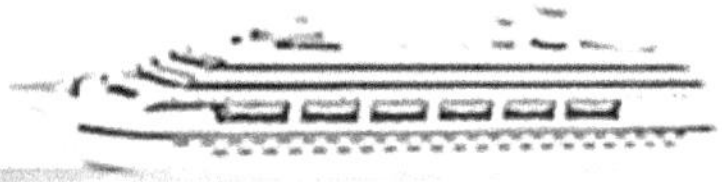

Draw a cruise ship

Colour the picture

Tuned into Cruising — Cindy's Journal Entry Two

Dear Journal,

Today, mom walked into the room, checking what I have packed; she jokingly started singing 'cruising queen' with the handle of the broom. I asked mom, 'wow mom, are you seriously going to sing ABBA right now!'. Mom changed the lyrics, which had me laughing in hysterics. The tune plays in my head, even now whilst writing in my journal on my bed.

Humming, I repeat her words, in tune with the whistling birds.

Cindy, I love your beachy clothes, something to be seen. You will now look more like a cruising queen.

A country girl, only thirteen, seeking to be a summer queen. From the farming breeze to a mood of the high seas.

You will board, explore and meet new friends. You can go to the kids' club, swim, play lots of sports, or just dance to all the music trends.

You will hear karaoke, dance and sing to the hokey pokey.

Having so much fun playing games to win a highlighter prize. Ooh, you will have the time of your life.

It is your holiday, my Cindy Bean, for you are the cruising queen.'

I ended up grabbing the broom and told mom to get out of my room. She was so embarrassing, and her song version was lame, but I told her that I love her all the same.

After all the excitement, I can not relax, as tomorrow the shuttle is coming, and I am hyped to the max. I am filling in my time, not being able to sleep knowing that tomorrow I will be in my holiday prime.

This is my family's first cruising holiday. So, I googled the cruise lingo that I may hear people say.

Colour the picture

I sit here finding that I am adopting my parents' puns. It is quite hard to admit that they are full of fun. For it is the night before cruising, and everything can get extra exciting, but also ever so confusing.

Cruising Life; Thanks for today, tomorrow is my holiday!

ESCAPE ROOM #2
Enter if you dare
Unlock Cindy's journal

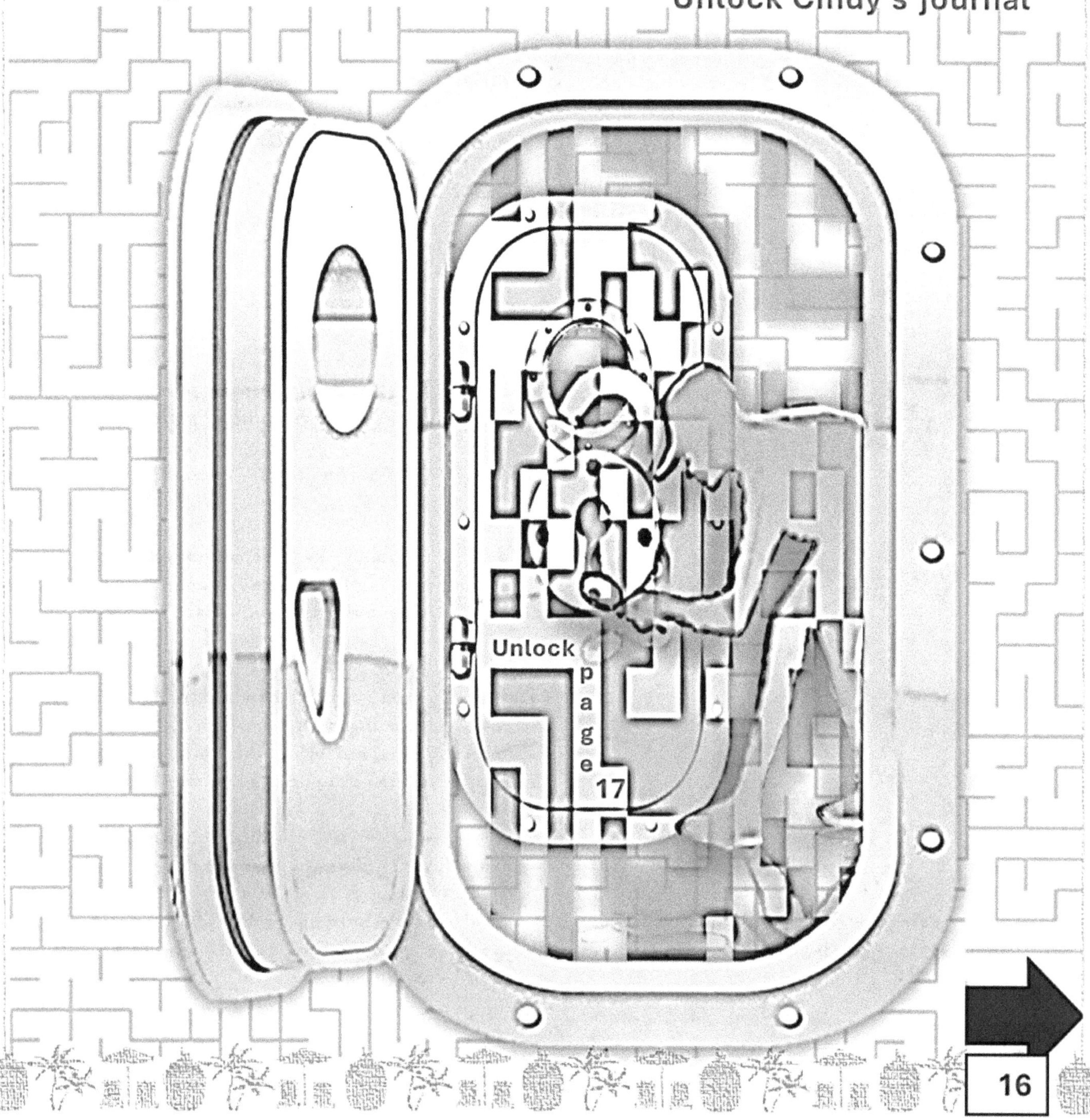

Unlock page 17

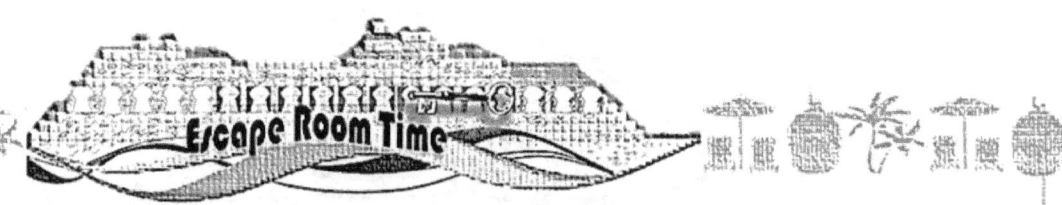

Escape, but don't make a mistake!

Oh no Cindy's journal is locked. You must solve puzzles to get out and through each section of her adventures before the ship docks.

What am I? Riddle me knot.

I will use keys, but I cannot open locks. I travel the world in cruise control, taking a rest, by using docks?

S _ _ _

I move along the sea without a deck, I sail with no crew, yet I help guide a ship, sometimes causing a wreck. I pass you by, but I don't smell. You cannot see me, but I am a big part of the sea and a cruise ships life. I may be blamed for effecting the tides.

W _ _ _

I will say hello and goodbye to you, but I cannot speak to anyone, even the crew. I sometimes dance and rock the boat (ship), but I don't have arms or legs to keep you afloat. I am mostly calm and sit low, but I can also get angry after a big blow.

W _ _ _

Each answer has something in common with each other. They all have _ _ _ _ _ _ _ _ _ _ _ ?

The shaded part will reveal the code that unlocks Cindy's journal and the pathway to her activities. Write the code in the box below.

Also, write the code on page 103

Answers on page 142

Activity Time

There are many cruise companies here and afar. Can you solve these rebus puzzles to see who some of them are.
(Rebus puzzles are pictures that represent individual words or phrases).

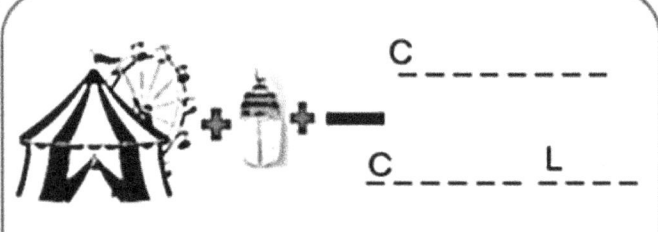
C _ _ _ _ _ _ _ _
C _ _ _ _ _ _ L _ _

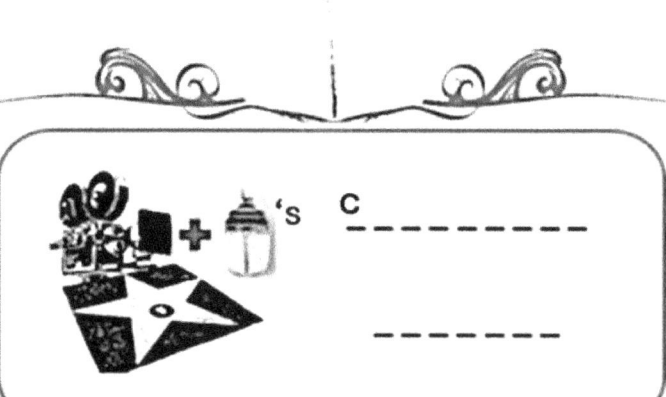
C _ _ _ _ _ _ _ _ _
_ _ _ _ _ _

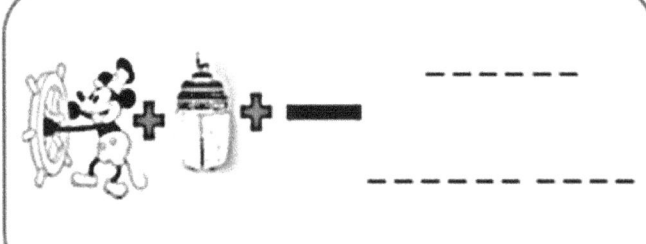
_ _ _ _ _ _
_ _ _ _ _ _ _ _

Crown + Caribbean Sea
_ _ _ _ _ _ _ _ _ _ _
I _ _ _ _ _ _ _ _ _ _

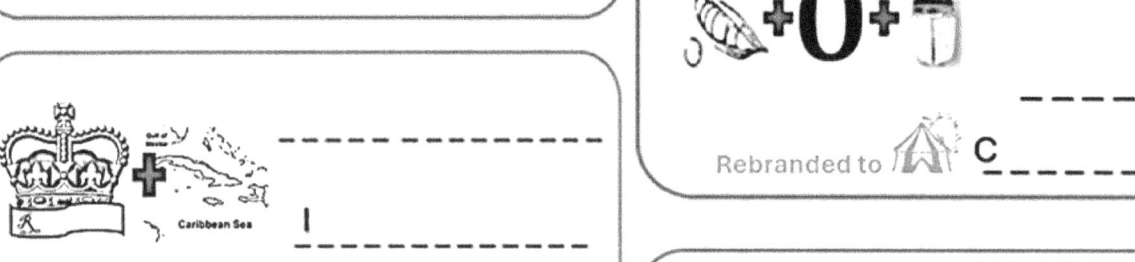
_ & _
_ _ _ _ _ _ _
Rebranded to 🎪 C _ _ _ _ _ _ _ _

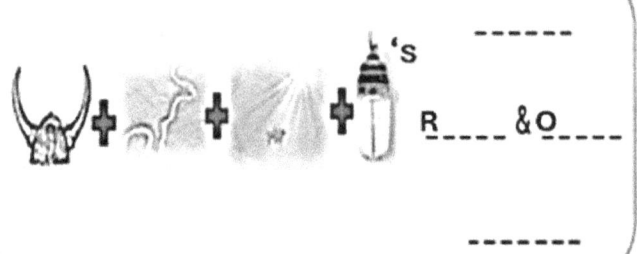
_ _ _ _ _ _
R _ _ _ _ &O _ _ _ _
_ _ _ _ _ _ _

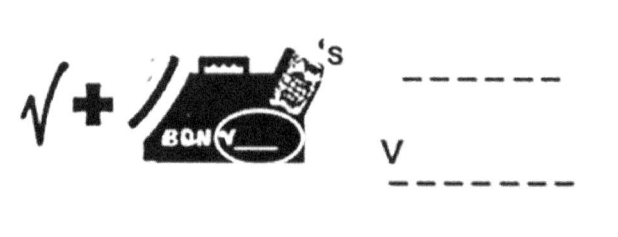
_ _ _ _ _ _
V _ _ _ _ _ _

Answers on page 142

Did you know?

A 'Ship Chandler'
Provides supplies, equipment, or maintenance, to ships all whilst at port.

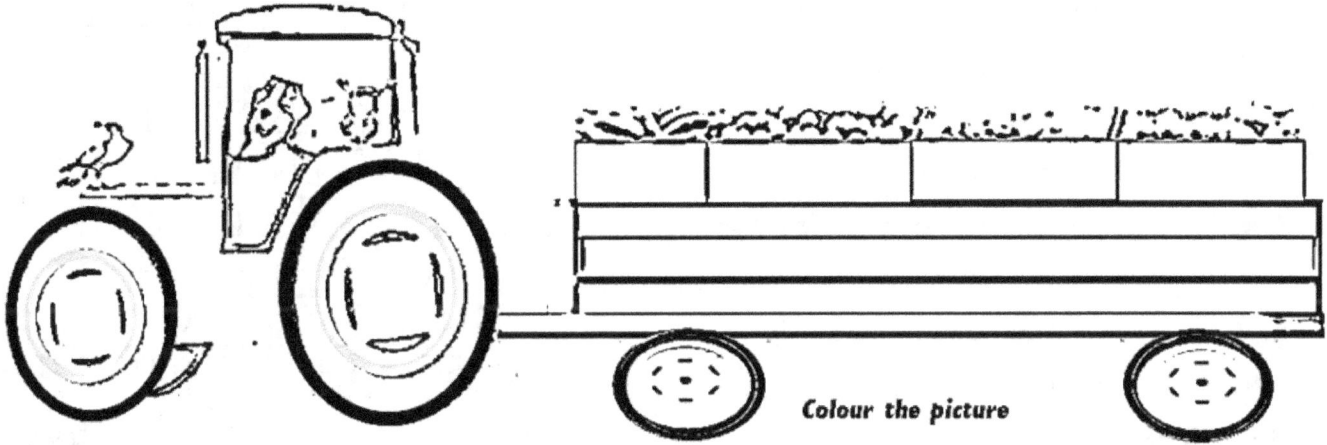

Colour the picture

Farmers seed, grow, and harvest crops as well as raising livestock. A very important role in supporting our livelihoods. The produce is transported via the Ship Chandler to the Cruise Ships.

The 'Cruisers'
Loves the land or the sea, but most of all enjoys life and feeling free.

Colour the picture

Nomads are people that travel to experience fresh pasture that may include their animals and towing caravans. There are also people that travel long-term on cruise ships, seeking fresh air and the love of the seas. Both have similar plans to feel the fresh air and breeze.

Before your trip, here is a little tip...
Decode some lingo and talk like a crew member. Look out, there are a lot to remember.

- ⚓ The central hub (main entrance) of the ship
- ⚓ A bed (in the cruise cabins), and known as the area where a ship is moored
- ⚓ The front of the ship
- ⚓ The location where the captain steers the ship (navigates)
- ⚓ The person that cleans your room and takes care of you
- ⚓ A card that is your room key, identifies you and is for payments
- ⚓ The person who is in charge of entertainment
- ⚓ Where passengers embark and disembark cruise ships
- ⚓ A daily schedule of activities
- ⚓ Going from ship to shore
- ⚓ Levels of the ship are called this
- ⚓ When you leave the ship
- ⚓ A place to moor the ship
- ⚓ Where ships go for maintenance and refurbishing
- ⚓ To go onboard the ship
- ⚓ The kitchen where the Chef's prepare your food
- ⚓ Walkway between the shore and ship
- ⚓ People tip the crew and staff for giving you a good service
- ⚓ The area of the bridge in which the steering is located
- ⚓ The outside of the ship, usually looks like a point
- ⚓ The bottom centre of the ship
- ⚓ Tie a rope in a ….. And a unit of speed at which the ship travels

Answers on page 143

20

Some more lingo, the line is as long as a Congo...

- The side of the ship where you'll be most sheltered away from the wind
- The deck where the pools are located
- When a ship visits a destination for the first time
- The first voyage of a new ship or destination
- The crew member responsible for the dining room
- The person who oversees the ship (the Captain)
- The main dining room onboard
- Middle of the ship
- A place where the ship is tied
- A mandatory safety drill that is carried out prior to sailing
- An assigned emergency meeting location
- The left side of the ship
- The crew member on land that will help you with your luggage
- Each destination you'll stop at for the day
- When main engines are connected to large generators to produce electricity (Azipods)
- The crew member in charge of onboard billing
- The process of sailing away from the shore
- A day at sea when your cruise ship does not visit a port
- Technology that keeps cruise ships motion to a minimum
- The right side of the ship
- The very back of the ship
- A form of transport to shuttle passengers to and from land when cruise ships can't access the port
- The trail of water created at the stern of the ship as it moves

CODES

| A | B | C | D | E | F | G | H | I | J | K | L | M |
| N | O | P | Q | R | S | T | U | V | W | X | Y | Z |

Answers on page 143

21

Who is who on the ship? That makes it a mega fun trip!
You may see some of these ranks around, take a basic look of who can be found!

Captain
The highest-ranking officer who is responsible for the overall ship operations. The Captain oversees navigation, ensuring the vessel's compliance, safety, and making decisions.

Staff Captain
Assists the captain, as the second-in-command, with managing day to day operations. They work together and the staff captain may also assume command in the captain's absence.

Chief Officer
Also known as the first mate, manages the deck department, inventory, and oversees the crew responsible for maintaining life-saving and firefighting equipment.

Chief Engineer
Oversees the engineering department. Responsible for the maintenance and operation of the ship's propulsion systems, engines, and other mechanical equipment.

Hotel Manager/Director
Oversees the guest services department. Manages the accommodation, dining, and entertainment facilities.

Cruise Director
Responsible for organizing and managing onboard entertainment, shows, events and activities. Supervises the entertainment crew. Makes sure guests are happy.

Doctor
Provides medical care, advice, and support to passengers and crew members in the event of a medical or health issue that may arise while on board. Also responsible for mandatory health and safety inspections and medical emergencies.

Food and Beverage Manager
Oversees restaurant, dining and bars. Manages menus, food, beverage, inventories. Ensures that a top-quality service to guests.

Guest Services Manager
Oversees the Guest/Customer Services, Customer Relations, Financial Controller, and Shore Excursions

Maître d
Manages reservations, schedules and supervises the food and beverage service staff, and waiters

Guest/Customer Services/Reception/Loyalty Ambassadors
Ensures guest satisfaction. Manages phone calls, cabin changes, lost and found, shore excursions, booking new cruises, complaints, service enquiries, cash exchange, guest accounts, administration, reception and broadcasting announcements.

IT Officers
Administer and maintains the hardware and software.

Entertainment Crew
Performs or directs activities for onboard entertainment. May also include performers, musicians, singers, dancers, entertainers.

Chief Steward/Stewardess
Stewardesses are responsible for maintaining cleanliness and uniformity in all areas, including the guest cabins. Chief Steward supervises the housekeeping department and ensures all guest needs are met.

Deck Crew
Supports with maintenance and operations. Assists with mooring, anchor handling, and deck equipment maintenance. They also help with emergency procedures and passenger safety.

Farm to the Palms **Cindy's Journal Entry Three**

Dear Journal,

Today, my 7 AM alarm blared, I almost snoozed it, until I realised it was time to get up because our cruise day was finally here!

Dad ran around like a headless chicken, making sure we had packed everything.

The Shuttle bus was finally here, waiting for everyone to get in. It was so cool, as an adventure was about to begin.

Despite the cold, breezy weather, I was determined to have fun; farm life has taught me resilience and how to get things done.

The shuttle driver packed the suitcase pile, then he welcomed everyone on board with a goofy smile.

He tried to be a comedian like dad and mom, and it made our road trip an entire load of fun.

Eye spy was one game we played, all whilst we detoured roadblocks on the way. He made our trip go fast with trivia and cringeworthy cruise puns to fill in the day.

Cruising life; Thanks for today, I am on my way!

Colour the picture

Story continues Page 35

ESCAPE ROOM #3
Enter if you dare
Unlock Cindy's journal

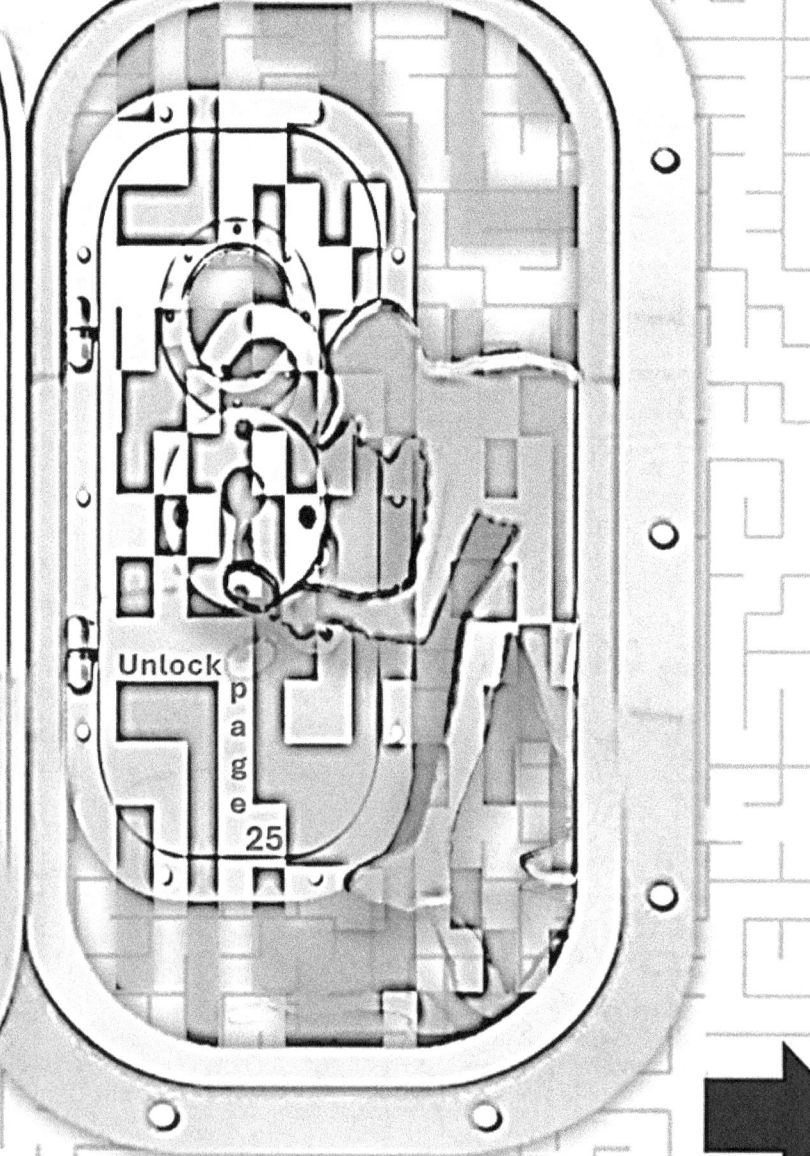

Unlock page 25

Escape, but don't make a mistake!

Oh no Cindy's journal is locked. You must solve puzzles to get out and through each section of her adventures before the ship docks.

Puzzle GRID

1	2	3	4	5	6	7	8	9	10	11	12	13
A	B	C	D	E	F	G	H	I	J	K	L	M

14	15	16	17	18	19	20	21	22	23	24	25	26
N	O	P	Q	R	S	T	U	V	W	X	Y	Z

Puzzle ANSWER

__ __ __ __ __ __   __ __ __ __
5 19 3 1 16 5   18 15 15 13

__ __ __ __ __
20 8 18 5 5

Write the letters that are under the numbers from the grid onto the puzzle answer. This will reveal the code number that unlocks Cindy's journal and the pathway to the next activities. Write the code in the box below.

Also, write the code on page 103

Answers on page 143

25

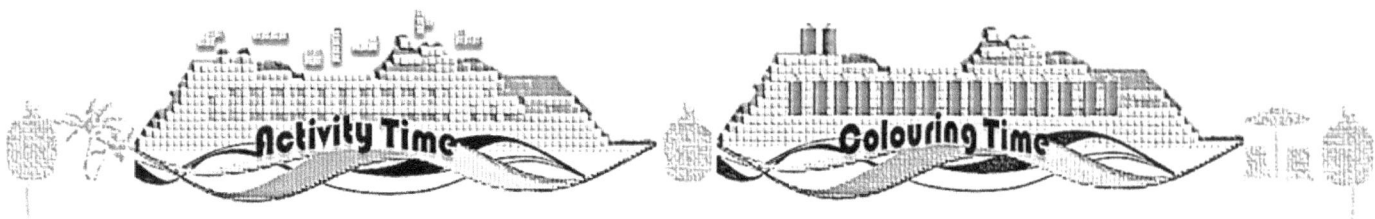

From the farm crops to the chef's skilled chop?

Thousands of kilos of fruit, vegetables, eggs, beef, chicken, pork, and lamb are loaded onto the ships.

The farmers are not just important to you for everyday living, but also on your cruise vacations, where they are forever giving.

Thank a farmer!

National Farmers Day (October 12th) each year

Colour the picture.

On the ship, the crew may carve some fruit and vegetables to wow you. Why not carve (draw) here and show your artistic skills too.

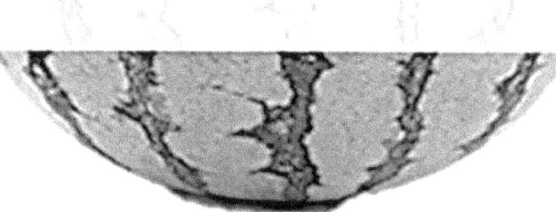

Carve your picture

26

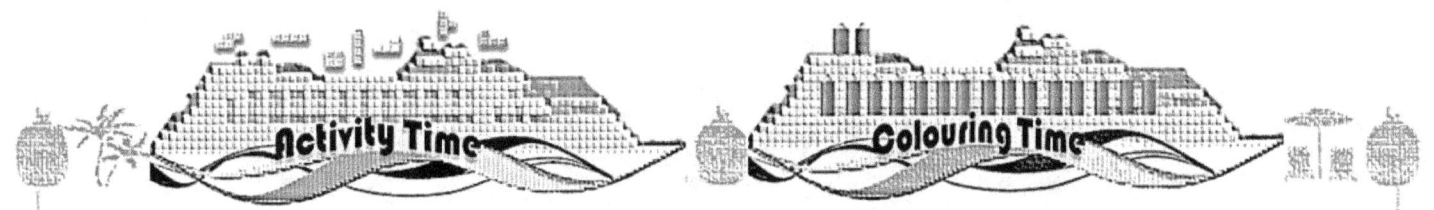

From the Farm to the Palms Road trip
I spy with my cruising eye....

Find & circle these items that have stowed away onto the ship.

Farm Fun Fact

Pigs are nosy, clever, and social animals who like to explore, eat and play. Pigs don't have sweat glands, so they must roll in mud to keep cool and prevent sunburns during the day.

Passenger Safe Fact

You will sweat from the blistering heat, so you will enjoy the pool on the ship, and beach on the shore. But to keep safe from the sun and prevent sunburn, you will need to put on sunscreen, a hat and maybe more.

Answers on page 143

27

These Ship jokes will make you laugh for Shore!
The shuttle driver loves to tell lots of dad jokes during your tour.

What did the students get on the cruise ship?
Answer:

What did the beach say when the tide came in?
Answer:

The cruise ship is fully booked but there isn't a single person on board. How?
Answer:

How do you disembark before even embarking onto a cruise ship? You have not boarded yet!
Answer:

What is the name of the optometrist on a cruise ship?
Answer:

Where do you take a sick cruise ship?
Answer:

Why did the cruise ship leave the port early?
Answer:

What medication did the doctor give to the Captain?
Answer:

What game is played every 100 years on a cruise ship?
Answer:

What do a fleet of cruise ships have in common?
Answer

What did the ocean say to the cruise ship?
Answer:

Why did the Captain cancel the trip to the Bluetooth iceberg?
Answer:

Where does a cruise ship get fuel at sea?
Answer:

What do the sailors use to clean their noses when they have a cold?
Answer:

Why was the Captain too full to eat during a storm?
Answer:

How can you tell when the ocean is friendly?
Answer:

What type of cruise ship is the best to cruise with?
Answer:

What is another name for a fit cruise ship?
Answer:

What did the Captain say when he was asked why he wasn't leaving the port?
Answer:

What vessel won the tug-a-war game?
Answer:

Answers on page 144

28

Trivia!

Adults enjoy trivia on ships to make friends and have fun.
Some may think they are smarter than the average pirate, but realise they need to run!

Circle the right answer.

What would you be travelling on if you wanted to go on a holiday that has a kids club?

Yacht	Ocean Liner	Cargo Ship
Warship	Submarine	Houseboat

On what cruise line will you see Donald Duck?

Virgin	Carnival	Princess
Disney	P&O	Royal Caribbean

What Cruise has (had) the Wiggles?

Virgin	Carnival	Princess
Oceania	P&O	Royal Caribbean

A child is allowed to press buttons in the elevator, but not here?

Pool	Dining Room	Buffet
Kids Club	Casino	Music Hall

Who was the first ever "Godfather" of a cruise ship?

50 Cent	Justin Bieber	PitBull
Bruno Mars	Ed Sheeran	Luke Combs

What Cruise line has (had) Dr. Seuss?

Virgin	Carnival	Princess
Oceania	P&O	Royal Caribbean

What is the busiest cruise port?

Sydney	New York	Miami
Santorini	Dover	Nassau

What cruise ship is taboo (not talked about)?

Mothership	Friendship	Warship
Carriership	Titanic	Cargo Ship

What is the brig on a ship?

Jail/Gaol	Kitchen	Cabin
Toilet	Bridge	Bar

Which feature on a ship may be fake/not used?

Engine	Anchor	Lines/ropes
Captain	Food	Funnel

Some cruise ships are missing this deck number?

One	Three	Five
Eight	Thirteen	Eleven

What are some toilets called on ships?

Brigs	Galley	Dish
Heads	Bridge	Flush

Answers on page 144

Are we there yet!

Oh no, there are road works, and your GPS has stopped. To get to the Port, you will need to help your family get through all the roadblocks. Start at 1A and finish at 13D.

Maze

Follow the road

- - - -

Watch out for the roadblock signs

	1	2	3	4	5	6	7	8	9	10	11	12	13	14	15
A	W (Start)	A	T	E	R	G	M	Q	P	O	B	S	C	B	Z
B	E	V	B	Y	J	O	B	O	A	T	W	H	E	A	T
C	A	I	R	K	W	N	I	B	O	A	T	C	O	S	U
D	T	V	G	S	E	A	G	U	L	L	O	D	C	H	R
E	H	P	M	H	N	S	T	O	P	E	R	E	O	N	
F	E	O	E	I	R	E	Y	K	W	F	T	R	A	P	S
G	R	R	M	P	O	R	T	H	O	L	E	I	N	A	P
H	J	T	D	O	P	K	S	D	E	C	K	H	A	N	D
I	P	I	Q	K	E	M	E	A	L	S	C	R	E	W	T
J	E	R	E	E	F	A	K	M	R	E	S	P	A	H	B
K	A	O	M	D	Z	P	T	L	B	R	I	D	G	E	U
L	R	A	O	C	T	O	P	U	S	W	A	S	H	O	S
M	N	D	Y	S	H	O	T	V	I	H	A	N	S (STOP / Finish)	S	E
N	C	L	I	F	T	L	D	O	C	K	T	O	U	W	A
O	S	E	N	A	Y	X	P	E	B	T	M	U	R	C	B

Answers on page 144

30

Are we there yet!

Answer is in the circled squares below

Fill in the Squares to see if you are at the port yet

Puzzles

1. CO-ORDINATES Check the Grid and write the letters to see what the message is. (view page 30)

2. SQUARES Write your answers, from puzzle number 1, into the puzzle squares. The circled letters will answer the question 'Are we there yet'.

3: MAZE - Trace along the road starting at the farm and ending at the ship. Watch out for the roadblocks! (page 30)

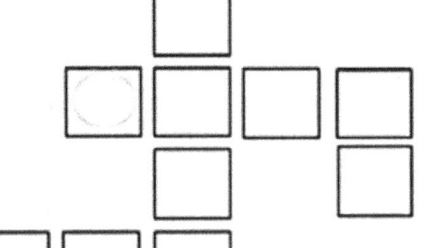

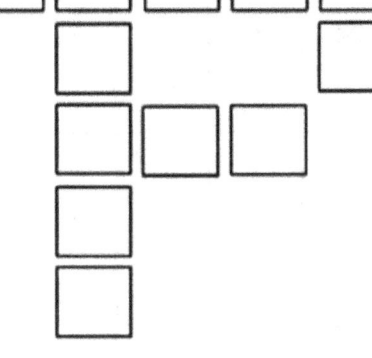

Check the co-ordinates to see the message on arrival to the Port

W												
A1	D5	K8	N1	E14	I6	J4	B15	H4	E8	E1	F6	

							A				
I1	L14	G2	M7	O10	M5	H9	G14	F12	B1	I8	

B11	M10	J10	J2	O2	B4	N8	K15	O4	I12	F3	

					T						
K1	A11	L3	N13	A3	I15	C9	O15	B6	J13	C3	M2

FUN FACTS
On the 8th of February 2005, the Google Road Maps was released. Prior to that the world used paper-based maps.

Did you know that on the 5th of April each year you are encouraged to go on an adventure the old-fashioned way and celebrate the Read a Road Map.

Answers on page 144

31

FIND A WORD

Find these words whilst travelling to the ship, it will keep you safe during your holiday trip.
After you have completed your road safety test, there will be 13 spaces left.
It is our message to you, before you venture into something new.

C	A	R	A	D	I	A	T	O	R	O	A	D	S
O	R	L	T	H	R	E	E	G	R	E	E	N	C
R	I	I	O	S	A	F	E	I	A	M	B	E	R
N	G	S	P	R	E	D	Y	V	S	T	O	P	O
E	H	T	B	I	K	E	S	E	R	U	L	E	S
R	T	E	E	N	J	O	Y	W	L	E	F	T	S
S	Z	N	T	I	M	E	O	A	S	L	O	W	I
H	F	W	A	T	C	H	U	Y	K	N	O	W	N
I	O	T	O	U	R	C	R	U	I	S	E	W	G
P	L	O	O	K	C	A	R	S	R	A	D	I	O
M	L	S	P	E	E	D	F	D	R	I	V	E	L
A	O	L	I	M	I	T	S	F	V	E	E	R	O
T	W	H	E	E	L	V	E	H	I	C	L	E	S
E	S	E	A	T	B	E	L	T	S	C	A	R	T

AMBER
BIKES
CAR
CARS RADIO
CORNERS
CROSSING
DRIVE
FOLLOWS
GIVE
GIVE WAY
GREEN

KNOWN
LEFT
LISTEN
LOOK
LOST
RADIATOR (not for page 33)
RED
RIGHT
ROADS (not for page 33)
RULES
SAFE

SCAR
SEAT BELT
SHIPMATE (not for page 33)
SLOW
SPEED LIMITS
STOP
THREE
TIME
TOP
TOUR
TRAFFIC

VEER
VEHICLES
WHEEL
WATCH
YELLOW
ZEBRA

Write hidden message here

Answers on page 145

32

FIND A WORD CAR SAFETY FILL-A-WORD ACTIVITY
Use the words from the fill a word puzzle

- _ _ _ _ down when passing emergency vehicles and pull out of the way when they need to pass.
- A safe driver always _ _ _ _ _ _ the road rules.
- Keep a safe distance from _ _ _ _ _ _.
- You must always adhere to the road _ _ _ _ _.
- Maps are good to use as they prevent you from getting _ _ _ _.
- A vehicle sliding on ice may _ _ _ _ out of control. It is important to drive to the road conditions, as it prevents injury and a permanent _ _ _ _.
- You cross the road using a _ _ _ _ _ /pedestrian _ _ _ _ _ _ _ _.
- If you go on a _ _ _ _ at a cruise port, make sure you are with a safe and licenced driver.
- When crossing the road, you should _ _ _ _, _ _ _ _ _ _ and _ _ _ _ _.
- Some countries drive on the _ _ _ _ while others on the _ _ _ _ _ side of the road, which also means the steering _ _ _ _ is on opposite sides.
- Always allow enough _ _ _ _ for your trip and don't rush.
- _ _ _ _ _ _ _ may mean that you slow down or stop to let another vehicle or pedestrian pass.
- There are three Traffic signals:
    1. _ _ _ light means stop
    2. _ _ _ _ _ or also known as _ _ _ _ _ _ light means slow down and prepare to stop.
    3. _ _ _ _ _ light means go.
- Watch out for the _ _ _ _ _ _ _ _ ahead, just in case they slow down or stop.
- Animals are _ _ _ _ _ to cross the roads, keeping an eye on your surroundings will help everyone in the _ _ _.
- _ _ _ _ yourself a break, stop and refresh during long distance trips.
- A _ _ _ _ sign means all cars must stop completely and then proceed when it is _ _ _ _.
- For safety of all road users, you must obey the _ _ _ _ _ _ _ _ _ _ _.
- Never have the _ _ _ _ _ _ _ _ turned up loud as you may not hear emergency vehicles or keep on _ _ _ of your surroundings.
- It is suggested to leave a _ _ _ _ _ second distance between cars.
- All passengers must wear a _ _ _ _ _ _ _ _ as it keeps you safe.
- It is always good, if you are a child, to watch adults _ _ _ _ _, as this will help you when you go for your licence.
- It is safer to slow down when you go around _ _ _ _ _ _ _.
- You must obey _ _ _ _ _ _ _ controllers

Answers on page 145

33

An anchor full of cruising

The anchor needs some colour so why not give it a little wonder

Colour the picture

Welcome aboard Cindy's Journal Entry Four

Dear Journal,

We finally arrived at the port; the ship was ready for everyone to board. I took a quick selfie on the grass in front of the ship, standing proud with friends and family, joining me on this glorious trip.

We joined the line to hand over our bags. Luckily, we had them all tied with our cruising tags. We went up the escalators and through the long lines. It felt like we were in a cattle muster whilst going through at our allocated times.

We had to obey the instructions from customs, staff, and crew. Once on board, we also completed the muster drill. I got to walk around and explore each deck and the city view, as the rooms were not ready until after two.

The buffet was open for a yummy feast meal. There was so much food, I had to pinch myself to see if it was real.

I went directly to the lido deck, where the swimming pool was located; however, after consuming ice cream and cookies, I waited a little while to avoid entering the pool with my stomach being so full. There were kids everywhere and a band playing sail-away songs. Looking around, I got caught up in the moment, and I nearly left behind my flip-flop thongs.

After we sailed away, a welcome-aboard colourful balloon drop happened inside. Adults were trying to sing, and if I were judging their sense of tune, it would take me a long time to positively decide.

Before going to bed, I pigged out on a lot of pizzas. This day has been such a blast, if only this evening had not ended, and it was going to last.

Cruising life; Thanks for today, we are cruising and on our way!

Colour the picture

Story continues Page 45

ESCAPE ROOM #4
Enter if you dare

Unlock Cindy's journal

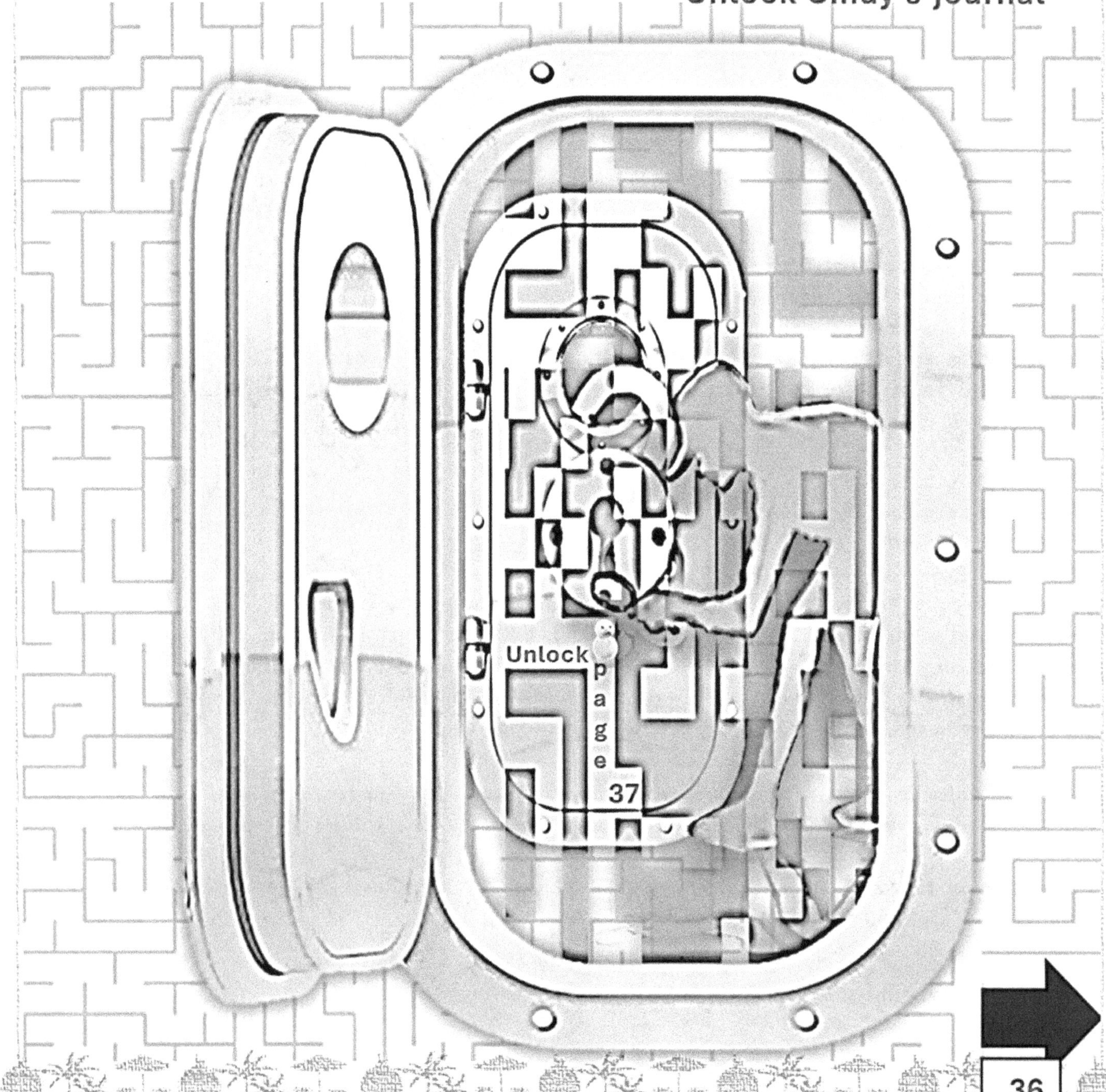

Unlock page 37

Escape, but don't make a mistake!

Oh no Cindy's journal is locked. You must solve puzzles to get out and through each section of her adventures before the ship docks.

Use the colour pattern below to match above

Solve the bubbler game to get the next code. Be careful to pop the right bubble by colouring the right pattern. There is a hidden number. Write the number you ended up with, in the box below.

Also, write the code on page 103

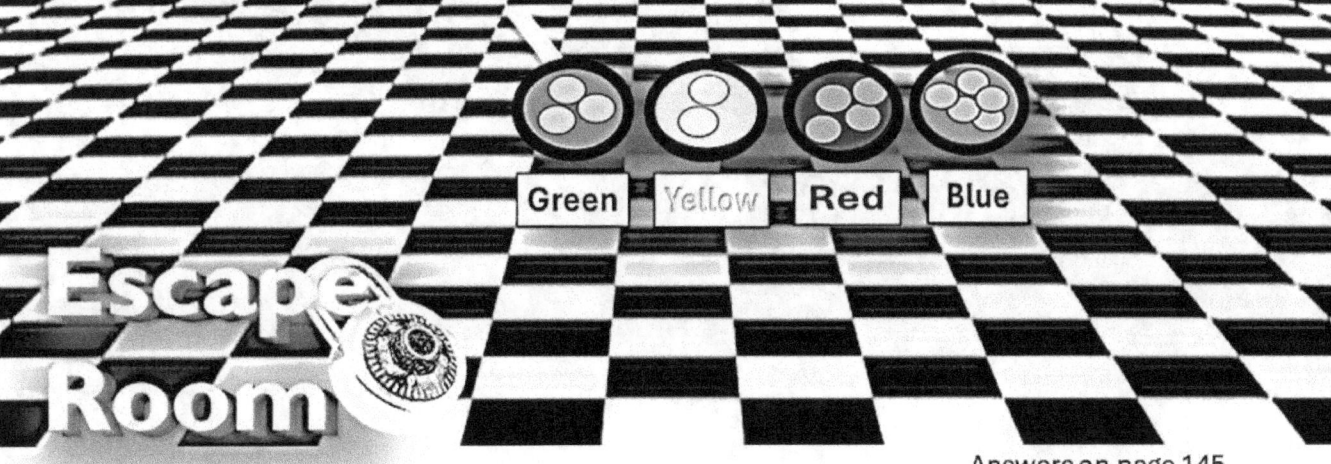

Green   Yellow   Red   Blue

Escape Room

Answers on page 145

Activity Time

To board the ship, there may be some things that you may need to complete...

Travel Ticket

PASSENGER NAME

SAILING DATES
Depart: __/__/__
Home: __/__/__

DESTINATION/PORTS

CRUISE SHIP NAME

TRAVEL TICKET
Boarding Pass

Fill in the spaces of the travel ticket

Sometimes you will need to go through Customs, and or, the check in queue.

For here it is an important place to protect the country, you, the ship, and its crew.

Customs scanning activity

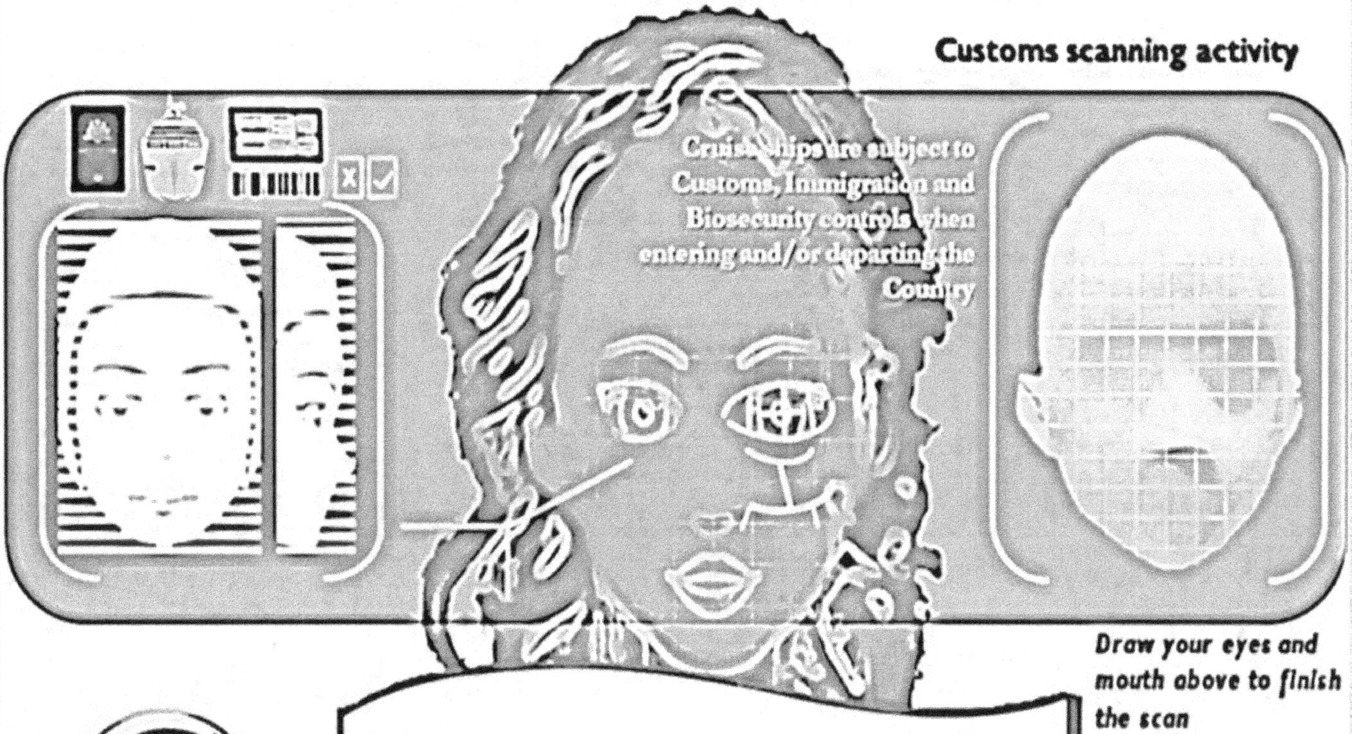

Cruise ships are subject to Customs, Immigration and Biosecurity controls when entering and/or departing the Country

Draw your eyes and mouth above to finish the scan

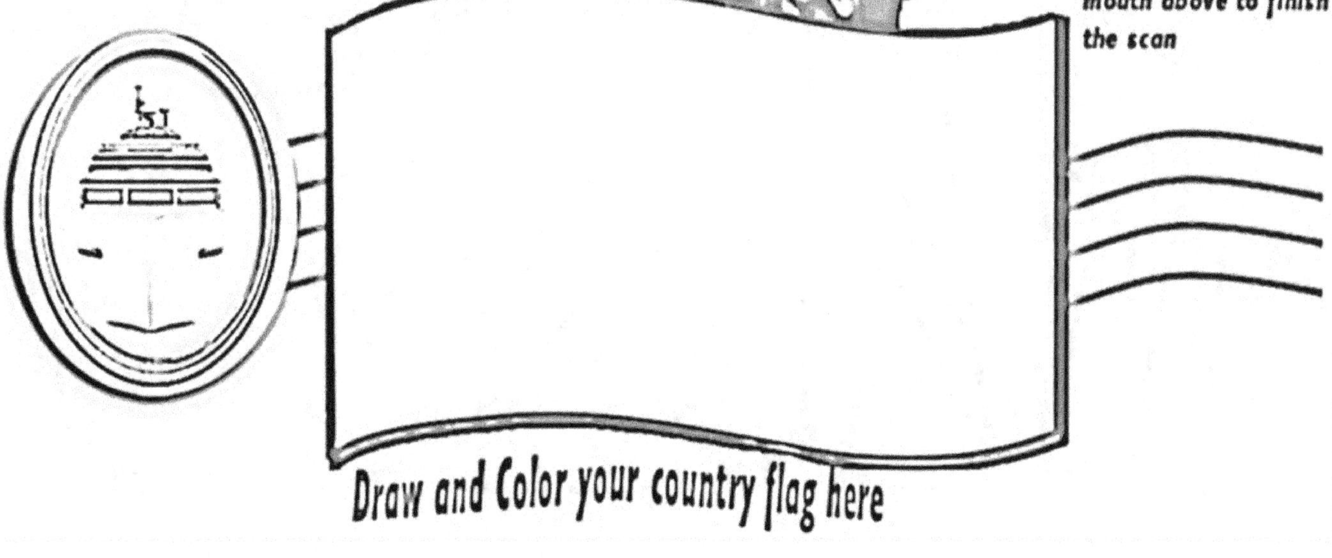

Draw and Color your country flag here

Colour the picture

Welcome Aboard Balloon Drop

The balloons dropping from the ceiling is a fun celebration, so lets put the burst of color back into the below ship's creation.

0	White
1	Grey
2	Blue
3	Light Blue
4	Red
5	Dark Blue
6	Black
7	Yellow
8	Orange

7	7	7	7	7	7	1	1	1	8	8	8	8	8	8	8	8	8
7	7	7	7	8	7	8	1	8	8	8	8	8	8	8	8	8	8
7	7	7	7	8	8	1	1	1	8	8	8	8	8	8	8	8	8
7	7	7	8	4	7	8	1	8	0	1	4	4	4	8	8	8	8
7	7	8	7	8	4	4	1	0	0	0	1	4	4	4	4	8	8
7	8	7	8	7	8	4	1	0	0	0	1	4	4	4	8	8	8
7	8	7	8	8	7	8	1	4	1	1	4	4	8	8	4	4	8
8	7	8	8	7	6	6	6	6	6	6	6	6	4	4	4	4	4
8	8	4	4	1	1	1	1	1	1	1	1	1	1	4	4	8	8
4	4	4	1	1	1	1	1	1	1	1	1	1	1	1	4	4	4
8	8	4	6	6	6	6	6	6	6	6	6	6	6	6	4	8	8
4	4	1	1	1	1	1	1	1	1	1	1	1	1	1	1	4	4
8	8	6	6	6	6	6	6	6	6	6	6	6	6	6	6	8	8
1	0	0	0	0	0	0	0	0	0	0	0	0	0	0	0	0	1
8	1	6	6	6	6	1	6	6	6	6	1	6	6	6	6	1	8
4	1	6	6	6	6	1	6	6	6	6	1	6	6	6	6	1	4
4	0	0	0	0	0	0	1	1	1	1	0	0	0	0	0	0	4
4	3	3	3	3	3	3	0	0	0	0	3	3	3	3	3	3	4
8	3	3	3	3	1	1	1	1	1	1	1	1	1	3	3	3	8
4	3	3	3	3	1	1	1	1	1	1	1	1	1	3	3	3	4
8	2	2	3	3	3	1	1	1	1	1	1	1	3	3	3	2	8
4	3	3	3	3	1	1	1	1	1	1	1	1	3	3	2	3	4
4	3	3	3	3	3	1	1	1	1	1	3	3	3	3	3	3	4
5	5	3	3	3	3	1	1	1	1	1	3	3	3	3	3	5	5
2	5	3	3	3	3	1	1	1	1	1	3	3	3	3	3	5	2
2	2	3	3	3	3	3	1	1	1	3	3	3	3	3	3	2	2
2	2	3	3	3	3	3	1	1	3	3	3	3	3	3	3	2	2
2	2	5	3	3	3	3	1	1	3	3	3	3	3	5	2	2	2
2	2	5	4	3	3	3	1	1	3	3	3	3	4	5	2	2	2
5	2	2	5	4	4	4	1	1	4	4	4	4	5	2	2	5	5
5	5	5	5	5	4	4	4	4	4	4	4	5	5	5	5	5	5
5	5	5	5	5	5	5	4	4	5	5	5	5	5	5	5	5	5
5	5	5	5	5	5	5	4	4	5	5	5	5	5	5	5	5	5

Answers on page 145

Welcome aboard!
Be safe abroad. A definite place you will never get bored.

Ahoy!
A fun way to keep you safe, and a float like a buoy.

A muster drill is to show you what to do if there is a real emergency, it is not a joke or a thrill.

The muster station crew leaders will tell you about how to put on a life jacket, where the muster stations are and to keep calm, there will be no racket.

They will also explain other things about emergencies on the ship. This may be done in person or on an app, they will keep you well equipped.

```
S  M  U  S  T  E  R
A  D  V  T  I  M  L
P  J  H  A  P  E  J
P  A  K  T  E  R  W
R  C  O  I  R  G  C
C  K  M  O  S  E  O
G  E  T  N  O  N  P
U  T  X  S  N  C  P
L  I  F  E  K  Y  Q
```

Find the underlined words

Now lost within the vest

••••••••

Answers on page 146

42

Activity Time

Fill in the blanks using the words on the Bow.

L_____ are located at the _____ _____.

Additional jackets are at l_____ _____ and on board the l_____ themselves.

Life jackets come in _____, _____ and i_____ sizes.

Always check the _____ and size on the jacket label.

Also, make sure you watch the _____ d____ to know how to wear one.

It is time to keep you safe now.

Adult
Child
Infant
Life jackets
lifeboat stations
Lifeboats
muster drill
muster stations
weight

Answers on page 146

43

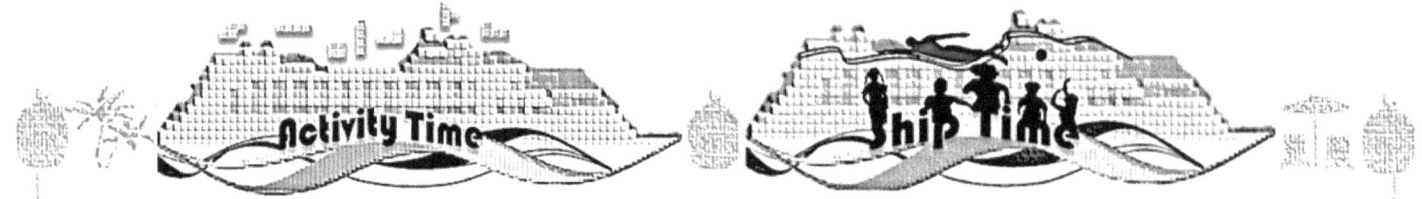

Making Friendships

Many people will cross your path while onboard, and some may even become lifelong friends once the ship is moored.

It's essential to treat everyone with respect and kindness, avoiding any negative remarks or slyness.

There are some people with disabilities but like you, they have many abilities.

Cindy has Autism which is a disability caused by differences in her brain. She may think in a different way, but her heart and soul are still the same.

Cindy may act, talk, interact, and learn in ways that are unlike you, but she can be happy and have fun too.

Cindy wears headphones, as she is sensitive to sound. When Cindy hears loud sounds, it can cause her stress and physical pain, so let's help her by finding what is around.

Write the deck number of where these sound events may be.

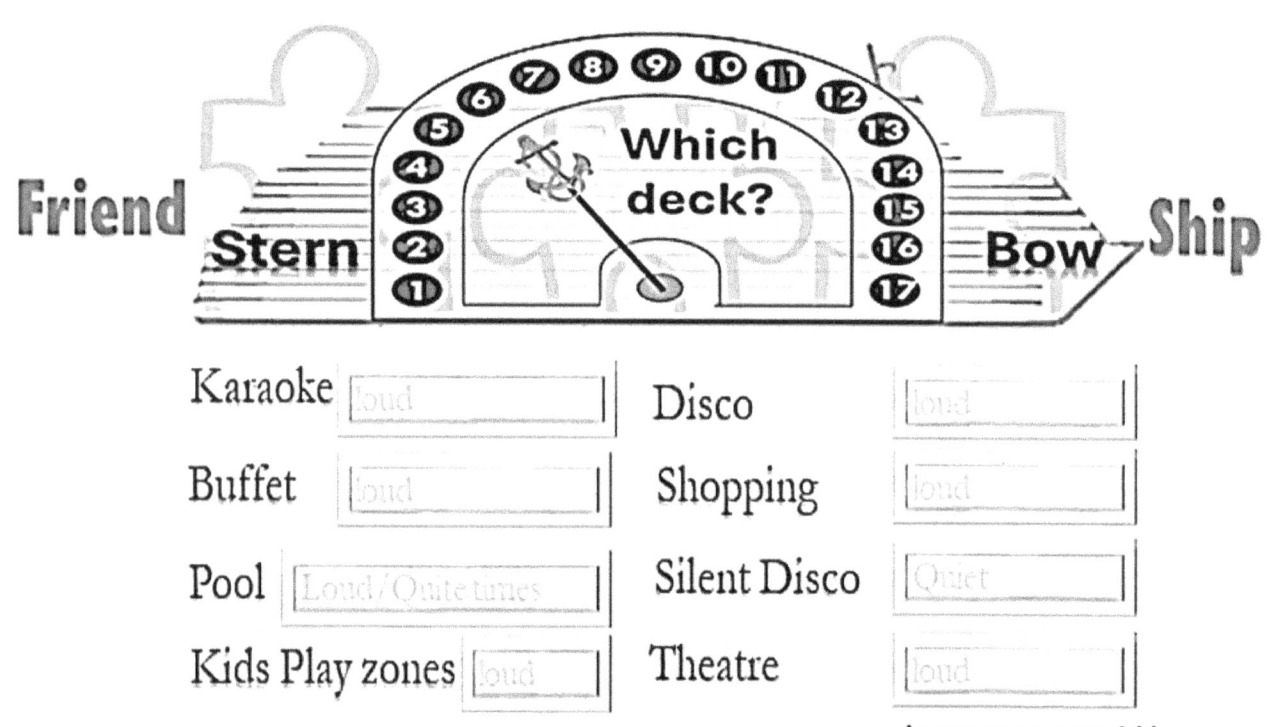

Karaoke [loud]   Disco [loud]

Buffet [loud]   Shopping [loud]

Pool [Loud/Quite tunes]   Silent Disco [Quiet]

Kids Play zones [loud]   Theatre [loud]

Answers on page 144

44

Seas the cruising way — Cindy's Journal Entry Five

Dear Journal,

There is so much to do on the ship. From the staff, I had received an important tip; to use the daily cruise planner to plan out my day, so I would not miss out on the activities or lose my way.

I looked at the cruise planner and seen that there are some sea and port days. I can go to the kid's club, arcade, and watch many shows or plays. There are also water slides, pools, and a basketball court. I also got excited when I seen that I can also play mini golf, as my chances are slim to shoot balls into that basket when I am so short.

I have realised that when cruising there's hardly any space to take time to pause, even the times when we arrive at the ports.

Even though this holiday is going to be a brief trip. I can still make many friends on the ship. While I am very shy and don't like the crowds and loud sounds, I still enjoy the cruising hype and having a friend around.

There are always new amazing adventures to explore, even if you have been cruising before. But this is my first overseas trip. I love seeing towel animals, the simple things that interests me, and even getting excited when thanking the crew for cleaning the cabin so quick.

On the farm I am always busy, and I spend most of the time with the animals and doing my chores, whereas here, I have never felt so dizzy. I have noticed that the ship sways, but I take tablets that help my legs balance and stay. It's fascinating to learn about the origins of the fresh food and water available, as well as the fate of any leftovers I leave on the table. To some, this is boring, but to me this is my calling.

Cruising Life; Thanks for today, a lot of activities, fun, and play!

Story continues Page 55

Colour the waterslide at sea

ESCAPE ROOM #5
Enter if you dare

Unlock Cindy's journal

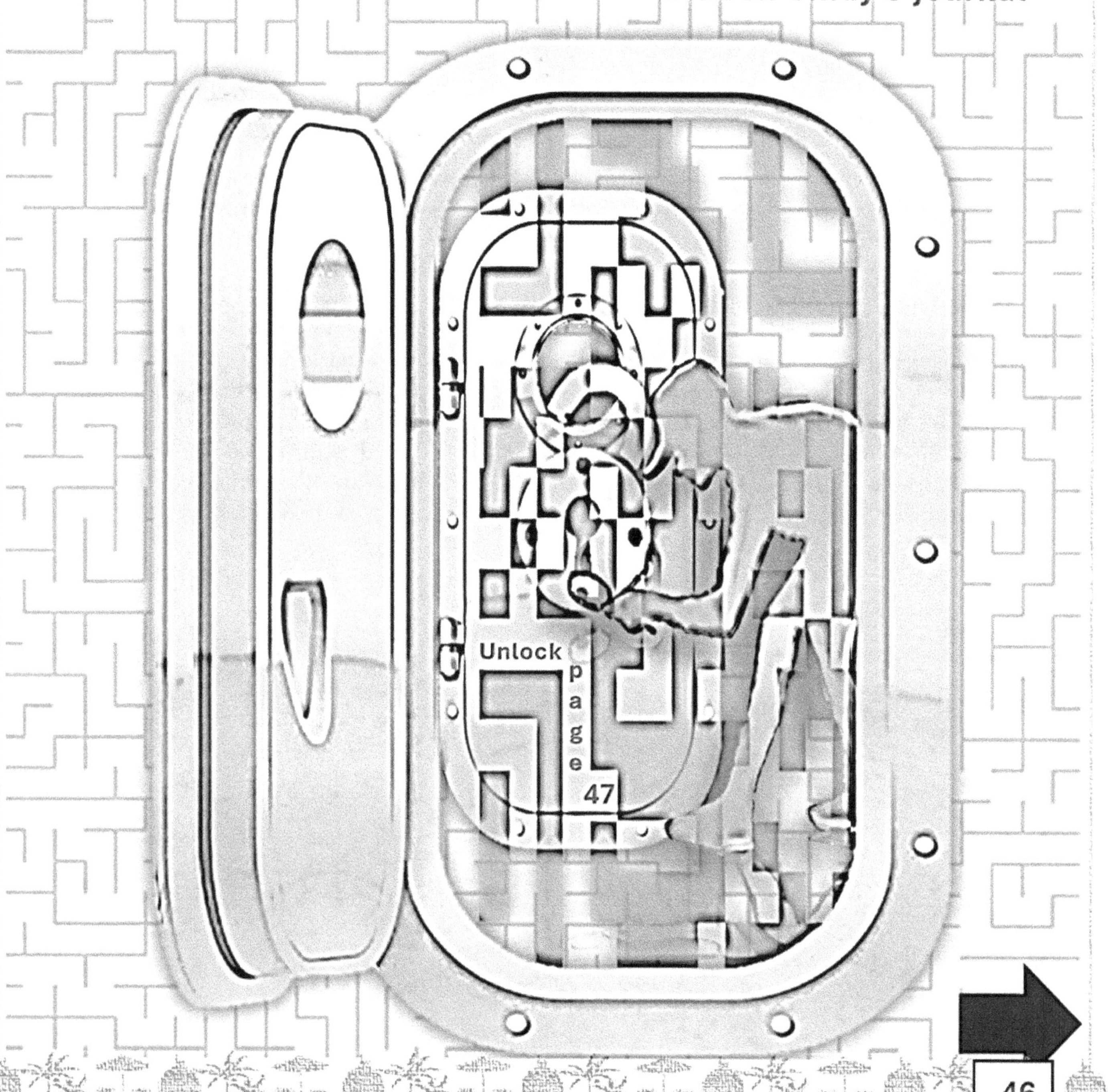

Unlock page 47

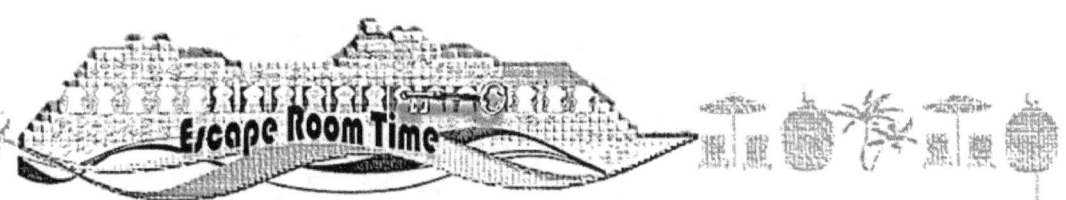

Escape, but don't make a mistake!

Oh no Cindy's journal is locked. You must solve puzzles to get out and through each section of her adventures before the ship docks.

Crack the safe in your cabin

1	2	3		None of these numbers are correct or used in any of the code squares.
4	5	6	A	Only one number is correct, and it is in the right place for the letter 'A' square
7	8	9		Only one number is correct, but it is not in the right place. It is used in the 'B' square.
3	0	2		Only one number is correct, but it is not in the right place. It is used in the 'C' square.
1	7	6	B	Only one number is correct, and it is in the right place for the 'B' square.
8	5	0	C	Only one number is correct and in the right place for the 'C' square.

A B C

Crack the safe to get the next code. Write the number that is in the 'B' box into the box below.

In this activity you will need to decode the correct 3-digit code from the hints on the left and then write them in the correct 'ABC' squares.

Also, write the code on page 103

Answers on page 146

47

Making Towel Animals

Cruise ship cabin crew may place towel animals in your room. Look out to see if it is on your cruise as there could be one anytime soon.

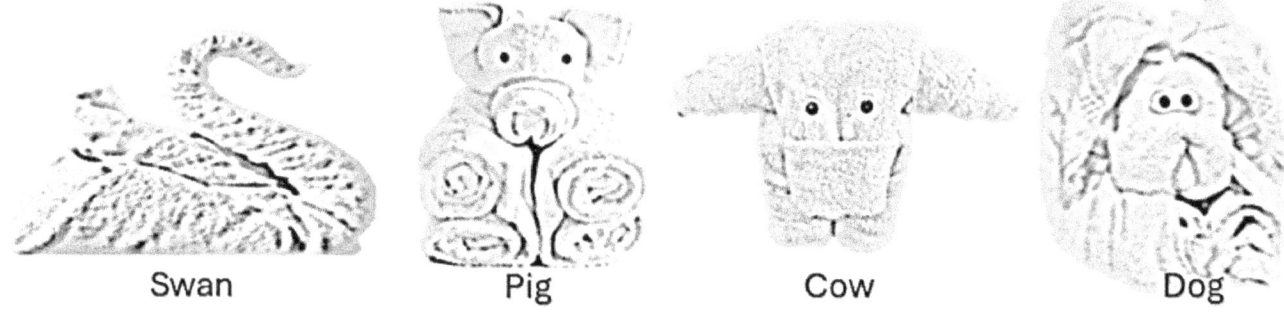

Swan Pig Cow Dog

MAKE A TOWEL **Ship**

Make a towel item

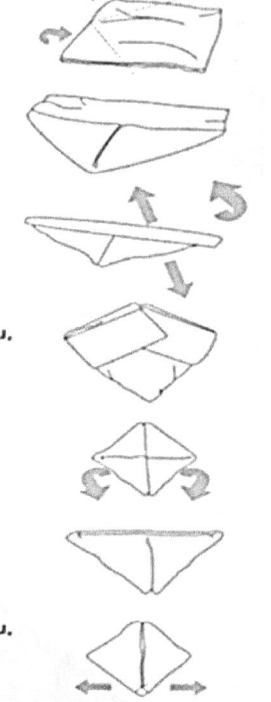

1. Lay hand towel flat. (Can also be made with full size towel).
2. Fold in half.
3. Fold ends of towel to meet as shown.
4. Fold bottom edge up toward point.
5. Turn towel towards you, pull out from center and refold.
6. Fold top point toward bottom point.
7. Turn over and repeat step 6.
8. Turn towel towards you, pull out from center and refold.
9. Hold bottom points, gently pull apart and flip.

Play a little game of Putt Putt and see which ball wins the cup.

Some cruise ships may have a mini golf course waiting for you to enjoy a little hit but watch out don't use too much force.

Find the number of shots it took to sink the ball into the hole, and the ball you used, using the Par for this course.

Par – the number of strokes (shots) you are expected to make to get the ball into the hole. This course is a Par 9 which means you should get the ball into the hole within 9 shots.

NOTE (HINT): The number of strokes it took to sink the ball in this game represented the <u>largest seabird</u>.

Shots ☐   Ball Sunk ☐

HINT – fun facts

Ace (Hole-in-One) – When you hit from the tee into the hole in a single shot.
Condor – four shots below par. On a par 9, you would get the ball into the hole in 5 shots.
Albatross (Double Eagle) – When you hit three shots below par. On a par 9, you would get the ball into the hole in 6 shots.
Eagle – When you hit two shots below par. On a par 9, you would get the ball into the hole in 7 shots.
Birdie – When you shoot one below par. On a par 9, you would get the ball into the hole in 8 shots.
Bogey – When you shoot one over par. On a par 9, you would get the ball into the hole in 10 shots.
Double Bogey – When you shoot two over par. On a par 9, you would get the ball into the hole in 11 shots.
Triple Bogey – When you shoot three over par. On a par 9, you would get the ball into the hole in 12 shots.

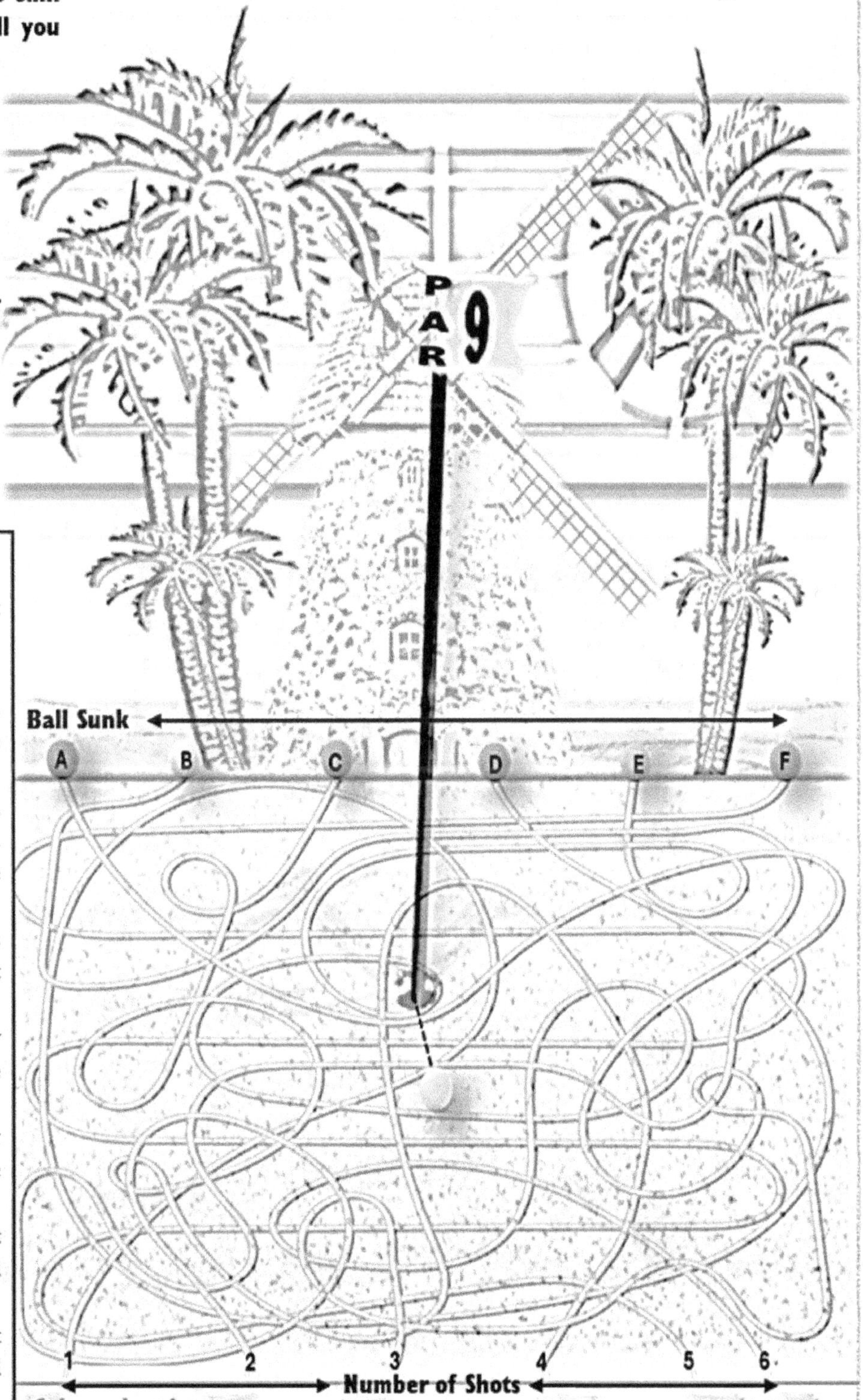

Colour the picture.   Answers on page 146

Slides and Ladders
Cruising is all that matters!

Rules

If you land at the bottom of a ladder, you can move to the top of it. If you land on the square with a slide, you must slide down to the bottom. Be aware of the seagull, you will have to go back 3 squares if you land on it. The first person to get to the space that says 'finish' is the winner and will slide down to the end.

No Dice

Play the scissors, paper, rock, ship, slide, and climb hand movements against your opponent. Take turns, and each outcome represents the number of moves you will get (dice value next to each hand). You cannot use the same combination twice in a row, and you cannot move if you both have the same gesture. Finally, you cannot win without using each of the hand movements at least once throughout the game. You can use either Auslan or ASL.

Scissors, Paper, Rock!
Play this game with a friend to see who is first to reach the top.

Ship, Slide, Climb!
Use sign language to reach the finish line in time.

 **SHIP**

 **SLIDE**

 **CLIMB**

Learning sign language allows you to communicate with people that may not hear at all or well. So, why not make the game even more fun and swell.

Slides and Ladders

Splash parks, pools, slides, and spas!

A floating City with a fun park ... Amazing! ... There's so much fun under the stars.

125 Finish	124	123	122	121	120	119	118	117
108	109	110	111	112	113	114	115	116
107	106	105	104	103	102	101	100	99
90	91	92	93	94	95	96	97	98
89	88	87	86	85	84	83	82	81
72	73	74	75	76	77	78	79	80
71	70	69	68	67	66	65	64	63
54	55	56	57	58	59	60	61	62
53	52	51	50	49	48	47	46	45
36	37	38	39	40	41	42	43	44
35	34	33	32	31	30	29	28	27
18	19	20	21	22	23	24	25	26
17	16	15	14	13	12	11	10	9
Start	1	2	3	4	5	6	7	8 End

Land on the square with the ladder and you can climb, but if you land on a slide, you will take a dive. Be careful, because when you land on the seagull, you will be sent back three squares to keep the game alive.

51

Just a drop in the ocean – fun facts

Water appears never-ending, yet it's just a drop in the huge ocean. A healthy future is important to us humans, as the ocean offers vital resources such as oxygen, food, and medicine to you and the crew men and women. Also, it provides avenues for recreation, exploration, and cultural identity, and most importantly, it is used on cruise ships, as there are plenty.

Bilge Water
Water that collects in the lowest part of the ship's hull, known as bilge water, which may contain oil, grease and other contaminants

Black Water
Water from the toilets that contains waste

Drinking Water
Water is either distilled from seawater or loaded onboard while the ship is in the port

Gray Water
Water created from showers, baths, sinks, laundry facilities, kitchens, and even water used in spas and pools

The floating city, (cruise ships), is self-contained, just like our farms & houses, where we all have a chance to recycle and retain.

Many cruise ships, have food waste controls through machines, that uses natural microorganisms to break down the food waste that makes it clean. The food is blended with water until it's a smooth mixture; and then either disposed of in port, incinerated, or pumped out to sea when the ship is in deep water and away from the coastline's fixtures.

On the land, treatment may be through composting, or by treatment plants, that allows the solids to settle and be removed from wastewater, like the cruise ship plans. Then a biological process is used to further purify waste liquid into drinking water, placing it all into a healthy drinking order.

Sea-ing that the water is pumped onto the ship, which tank will first fill to the top, as it tips?

**Circle the answer.
But watch out for the blocked pipes.**

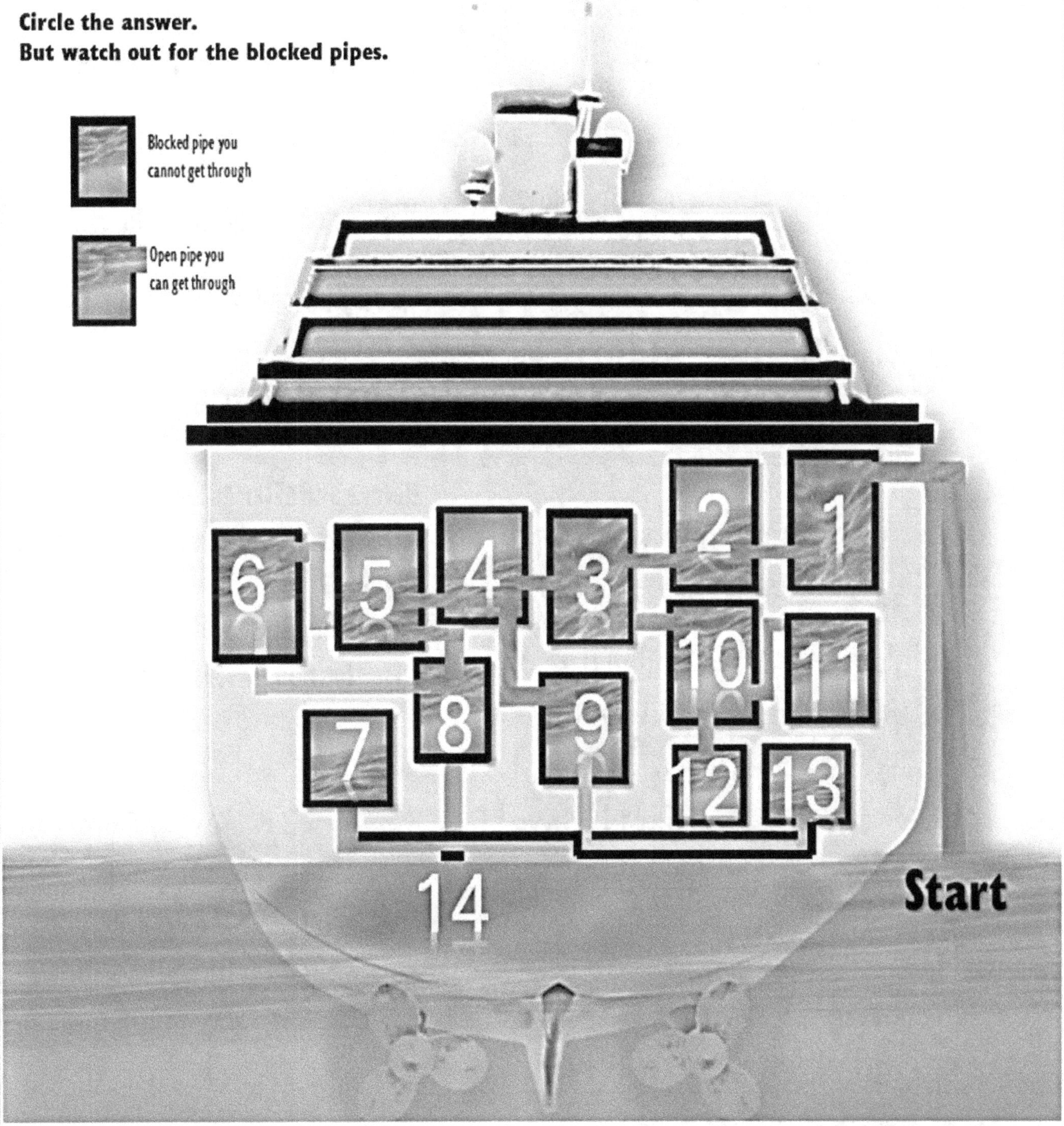

Answers on page 147

Activity Time

Help the crew clean the deck

All the germs are causing a wreck

Find and circle **6 differences**, and help Squiggly keep the cruise spick and speck

Washy, washy, scrub your hands.

Swishy, swishy, kill those germs.

Turn the water off and dry, dry, dry,

Off you go don't be shy, shy, shy

Be quick quick, quick,

to stop becoming sick, sick, sick

ALWAYS CLEAN;

- Before and after eating
- After blowing your nose Sneezing and coughing
- After using the toilet
- After touching doors/buttons

Answers on page 147

Balancing the difference Cindy's Journal Entry Six

Dear Journal,

My inquisitive mind is in full force, but the crew does not squint, or show being annoyed or having any remorse. The crew is helpful and gives me a load of answers. They are friendly and always happy to spend time with me, even if they are only chefs, stewards, or even the ship's dancers.

Some people cruise to visit different destinations, or even possibly they may simply like to enjoy, relax, which is all about the journey. But cruising is my holiday, which includes having fun, enjoying activities and learning.

One person teased me today, but it will not ruin my fun vacay. I've heard that some have defined me as weird, but I know my individuality shouldn't have me feared. My curiosity does not differ from others learning about fashion, cars, or celebrities on social media; it is just another outlet for my teenage energy, loving life through a walking encyclopaedia.

Today I let some energy out by racing around the running track. I looked out to the sea and watched dolphins surfing the waves in their packs. I found a friend who also explores ships, which is amazing, how many of us find our connecting clicks.

Despite the richness of less healthy options such as pizza, cookies, and fries, the fruits and vegetables will provide a nutritional counterbalance for my sugar highs.

We also went for a tour through the Galley and on the bridge. I found the technology high-tech and the ridgy-didge. I had so much fun navigating the high seas. It was all such a big tease. We are going forward on cruise control, with the Captain loving every part of his role. Like me, cruising is in our soul.

Colour the picture

Cruising Life; Thanks for today, a balancing act of fun and play!

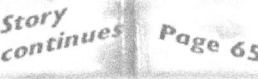

ESCAPE ROOM #6
Enter if you dare

Unlock Cindy's journal

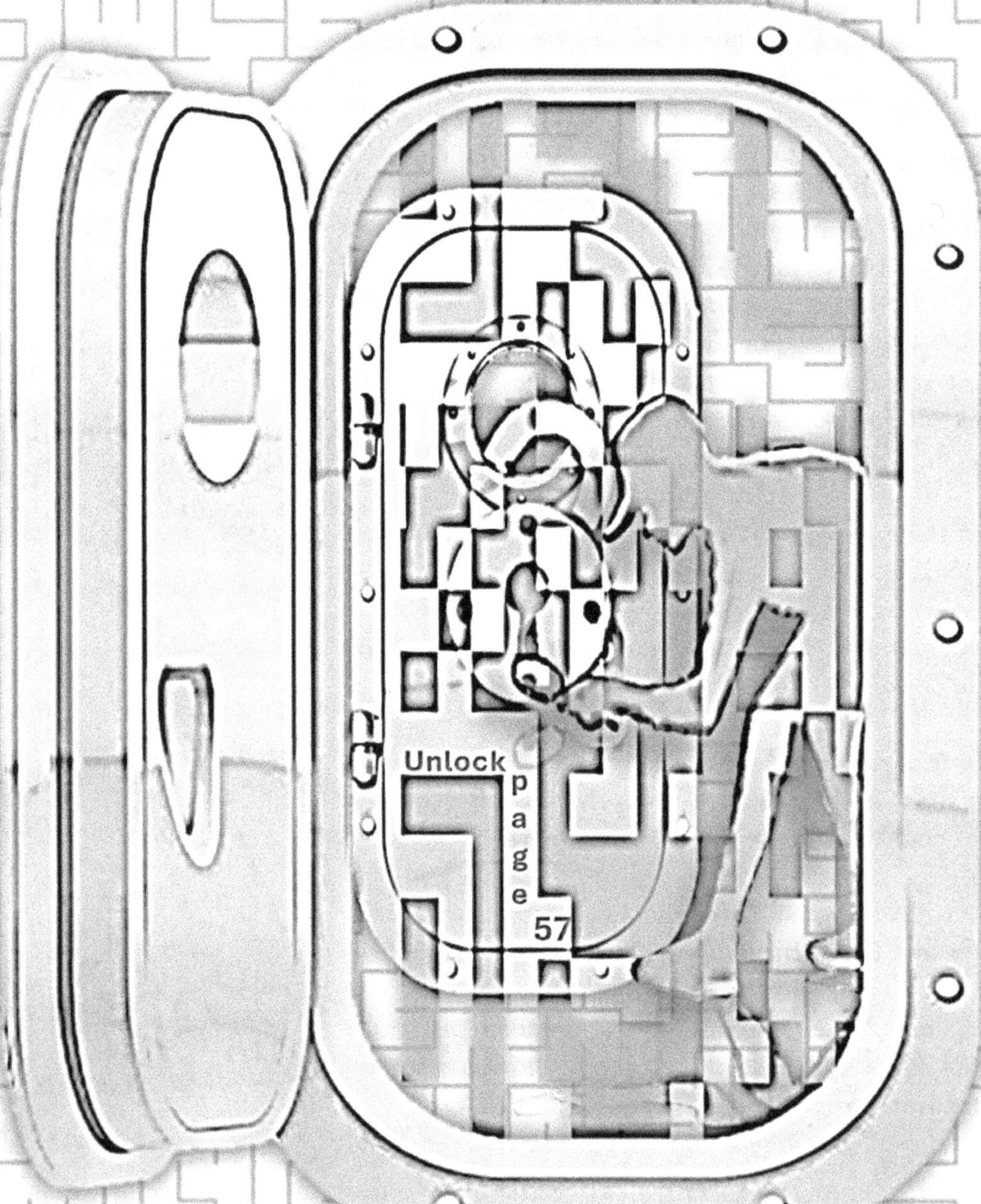

Unlock page 57

56

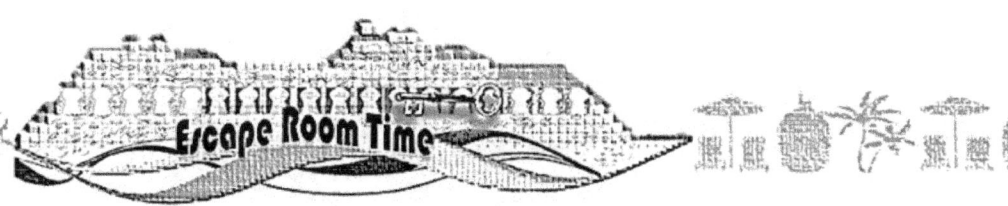

Escape, but don't make a mistake!

Oh no Cindy's journal is locked. You must solve puzzles to get out and through each section of her adventures before the ship docks.

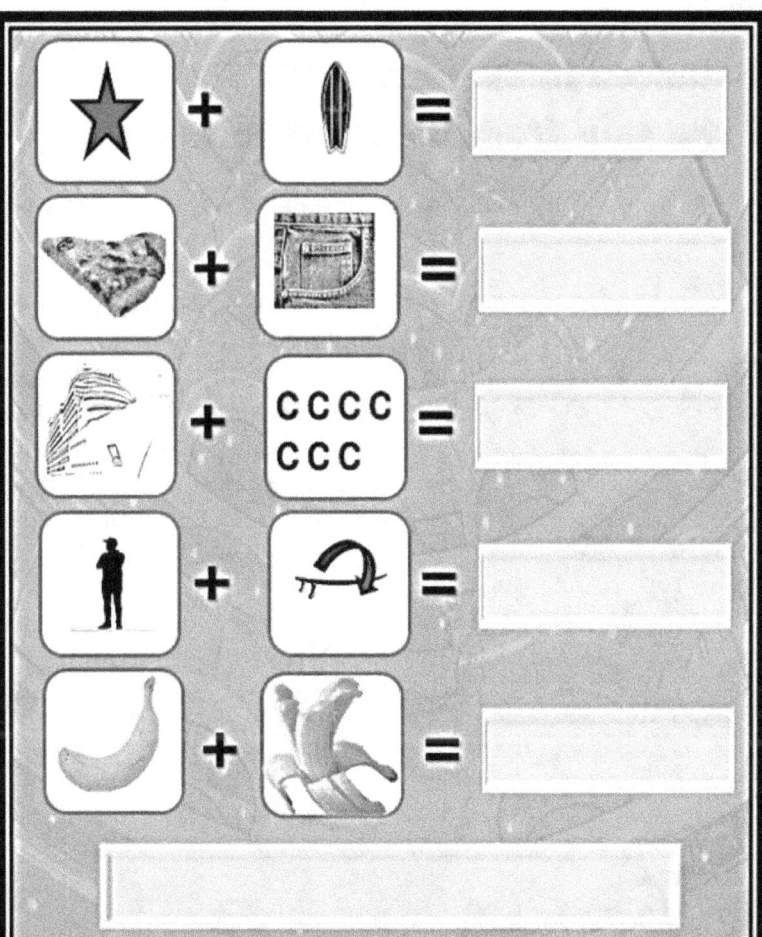

Decode the puzzle to reveal each word.

Each word in order has one letter that will join to spell a five-letter number to reveal the code.

Write the code in the box below.

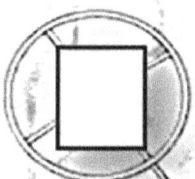

Also, write the code on page 103

Answers on page 147

Well, Balanced in every way, to help you and the ship from the many sways.

There's so much food on board, so to stop feeling so full, make sure you look after yourself, and balance your intake too!

Cruise ships are huge, and they can hold their heavy weight. The hull of a cruise ship moves thousands of tons of water, pushing it down and to the sides. The ship doesn't sink because the bulk of the water pushes back against the ship, keeping it afloat.

Have you ever noticed that cruise ships place their pools in the middle? Or that the spas or pools are balanced by having one on each side of the ship? Well, the whole ship is planned on balance. Giving you the most of fun and enjoyment. You may also see a pool emptied in bad weather; this may also be a tipping point!

Also, for balance, the cruise ships have a draft/draught. This is the depth of the ship below the waterline. The draft can vary depending on the weight of the ship at the time, due to increased displacement. Most ships have a draft of between 25 to 30.

The Cruise ships hull has ballast tanks which help with the stability of the whole vessel. They help modify the center of gravity by filling up with seawater. It helps to keep the ships afloat and stable, avoiding them from tipping over. Many cruise ships have stabilisers that assist during bad weather.

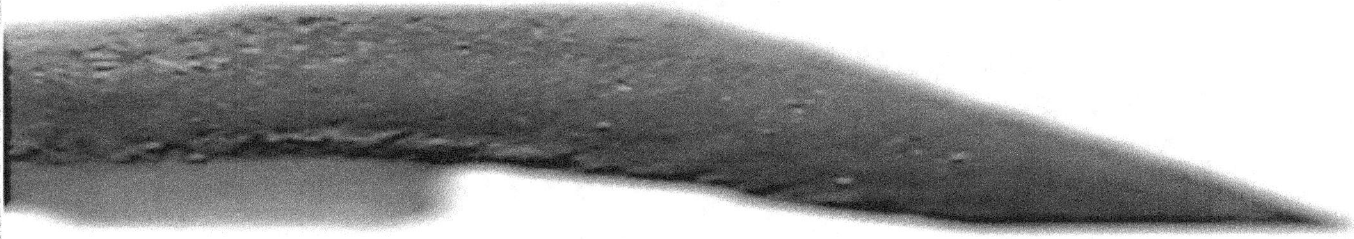

Activity Time

Balancing on the high seas

Clue	Answer
Fills up with water	BALLAST
Ship stability is determined by the balance between these two forces	BUOYANCY / GRAVITY
watertight body of a ship	HULL
Two fins that form part of the hull	STABILISER
Produced by cows	DAIRY
Mature and ripened ovaries of flowers	FRUIT
Edible seeds of plants	GRAINS
To build and repair muscles and bones	PROTEIN
Edible plant matter	VEGETABLES

5 Ship balancing acts
- Ballast
- Buoyancy
- Gravity
- Hull
- Stabiliser

5 body balancing facts
- Dairy
- Fruit
- Grains
- Protein
- Vegetables

Vitamin Sea

Place these into the above grid

Answers on page 147

A Quick Overview — Fun Facts About Cruise Ships

I kid your knot in cruise control!
One knot is equal to one nautical mile per hour

The fastest cruise ship in service today (2025) is Cunard's Queen Mary 2, with a reported top speed of 30 knots (56 km/h).

In the 17th century, sailors measured the speed of their ship using a device called a 'common log'. The common log was a rope with knots at regular intervals, attached to a piece of wood shaped like a slice of pie.

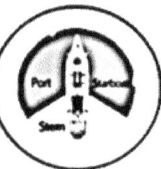

I am stern on what way to go!
Direction is key to getting around the ship.

Aft: the rear of the ship.
Bow: the front of the ship.
Forward: the front of the ship.
Midship: the middle of the ship.
Port: the left side of the ship, when facing forward (red).
Starboard: the right side of the ship, when facing forward (green).
Stern: the rear of the ship.
Topside: the top portion of the outer surface of the ship on each side above the waterline.

What ever floats your..................

Cruise ships are huge, and they can hold their own heavy weight. The hull of a cruise ship moves thousands of tons of water, pushing it down and to the sides. The ship doesn't sink because the bulk of the water pushes back against the ship, keeping it afloat.

Cruising to new heights!
The biggest cruise ship to sail as of beginning of 2025 is the Royal Caribbean's Icon of the Seas

Cruise ships are assessed based on their registered gross tonnage, based on how much inside space is on a ship (volume). They are also measured by length, and passenger capacity. Icon of the Seas has 21 decks, 7 pools and 9 whirlpools, including an infinity pool. It has the largest waterpark at sea with six waterslides. There are 8 neighborhoods, including an ice rink, aqua dome and robots. It is 365 long, with a gross tonnage of 248,663, and travels at a speed of 22 knots (41 km/h). There are 2,350 crew to make your trip memorable, serving a maximum capacity of 7,600 passengers.

Cruising the intimate way!
The smallest cruise ship to sail as of 2025 is the Celebrity Cruises Xploration.

The cruise ship has 3 decks accessible to the passengers and crew. The maximum capacity is 16 passengers. The ship has a gross tonnage of 320, a length of 98.3 ft, and it cruises at a speed of 10 knots (18.52 km/h)

Boat or Ship?..................................
Vessels navigating coastal and inland waters are mainly called boats, while vessels cruising through oceans are mainly called ships

Where am I?
DRAW A LINE TO THE CORRECT PLACE ON THE SHIP
Remember that these are not in the right position.

Bow   Starboard   Stern

Midship   Port

Forward   Aft

Match the directions and find your way, as you become excited to head to the kids' club to play. Complete both puzzles - the diagram above and the words below by drawing a line.

Aft	Front of a cruise ship, facing the bow.
Bow	Left side of the ship when facing forward.
Forward	Between the forward and the aft of the ship.
Midship	The front curve part of the ship that helps cut through water.
Port	Right side of the ship when facing forward.
Starboard	The rear of the ship. Difference between stern and aft is that the aft is onboard whereas the stern is the outside back.
Stern	Back of the ship, which is opposite to the Bow.

You may hear a lot of directions, and you may feel a little lost, but that is normal, as it would likely be because of the many decks and sections.

Answers on page 148

I CRUISE YOU KNOT!

Ships speed is related to the earth's degree of latitudes, and that is no crock!

Fun Fact: A knot is a unit of speed. The term knot comes from as far back in the 17th century, when sailors used a common log to measure speed of their ship. The common log had a piece of long wood (logline, drum and handles) with rope wrapped around it. The rope had knots at regular intervals, with a piece of chip wood at the end. The line is divided by evenly spaced knots which act as markers. The number of knots that slipped through the sailor's hand, indicated the speed.

A Seaman watched and counted how many knots in the rope have passed into the sea in each time. That provided the reading of the ship's speed in knots. One knot equals one nautical mile per hour (1.852 km/h). The larger passenger cruise ships may travel around 21 to 24 knots, which is 24.1664 to 27.6187 miles per hour (38.9 to 44.4 km/h).

Speed = Distance ÷ Time

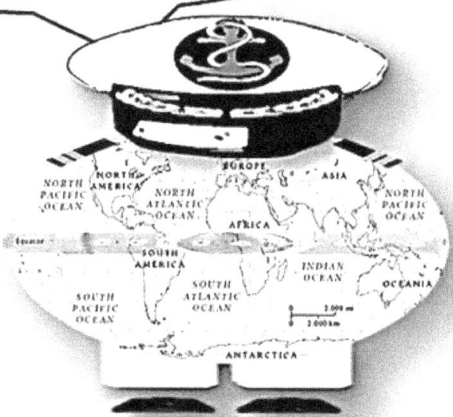

For the love of the high seas, advanced FACTS for those child captains to be!

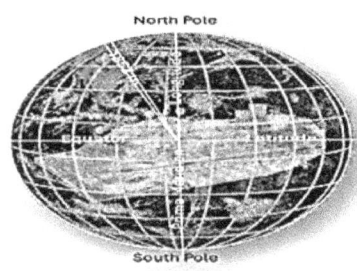

Ships measurement is related to nautical miles, which in turn is linked to the curvature of the earth. A nautical mile is the unit of length to measure distance. One nautical mile is equal to one minute of latitude. For example, if 3 knots slipped through the sailor's hand in 30 seconds, then speed of the ship was 3 knots. It meant that the ship covered 3 nautical miles in an hour.

I kid you KNOT!
Tie a line, practice with time, you will be a master, but watch out, there are a lot!

Fun Fact: A knot is also known where a single line (rope) is made into a shape, and it is then used for a purpose. Crew members have the skills in creating a hitch (attach a line to an object) and a bend (joining two lines together).

Can you become skilled in rope work and enjoy the trade of the seas? Continue your great crew member skills and work alongside the quays.

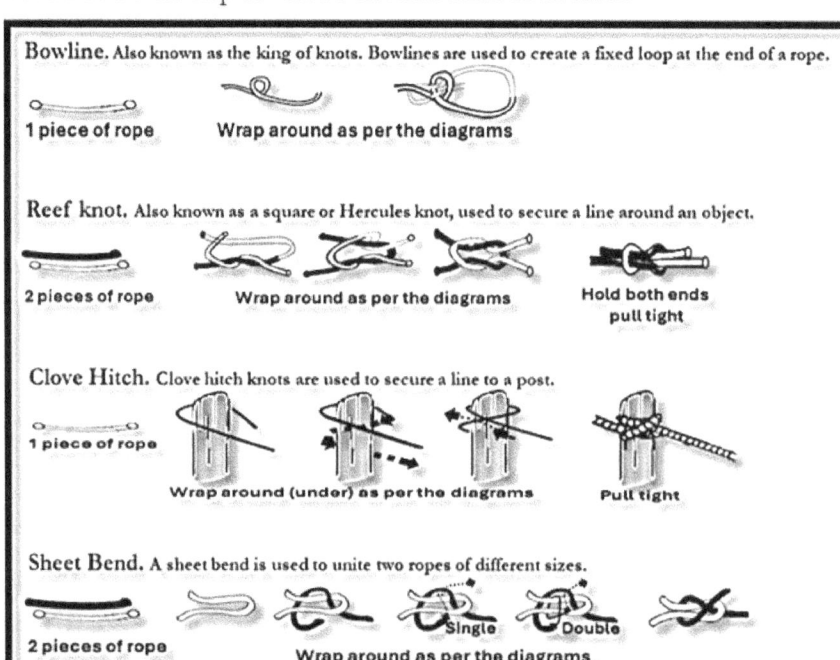

Bowline. Also known as the king of knots. Bowlines are used to create a fixed loop at the end of a rope.
1 piece of rope — Wrap around as per the diagrams

Reef knot. Also known as a square or Hercules knot, used to secure a line around an object.
2 pieces of rope — Wrap around as per the diagrams — Hold both ends pull tight

Clove Hitch. Clove hitch knots are used to secure a line to a post.
1 piece of rope — Wrap around (under) as per the diagrams — Pull tight

Sheet Bend. A sheet bend is used to unite two ropes of different sizes.
2 pieces of rope — Single — Double — Wrap around as per the diagrams

Information is limited and consists of a basic overview

Take the Con and navigate the way.
You are in cruise control, what else can we say.

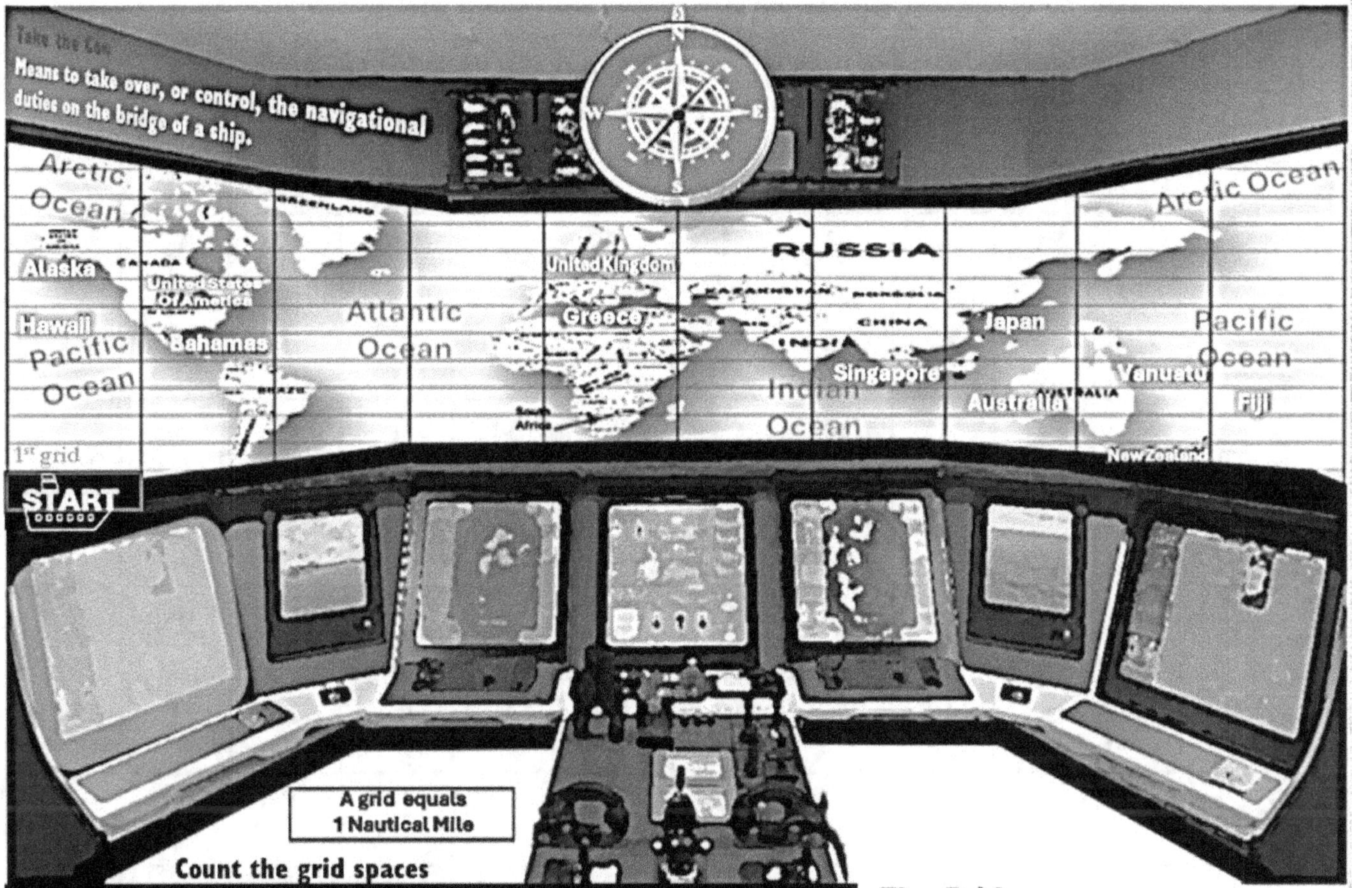

Take the Con – Means to take over, or control, the navigational duties on the bridge of a ship.

A grid equals 1 Nautical Mile

Count the grid spaces

COUNTRY destination (Written in the square)	Direction (only go up & across)	Nautical Miles (between both)
From Start to Hawaii	Head NORTH only	
Hawaii to Greece	Head EAST only	
Greece to Japan	Head EAST only	
Japan to Australia	Head SOUTH only	
Australia to Fiji	Head EAST only	
Fiji to New Zealand	Head SOUTH then WEST	
New Zealand to Vanuatu	Head NORTH only	
Vanuatu to Singapore	Head WEST only	
Singapore to United Kingdom	Head WEST then NORTH	
United Kingdom to Alaska	Head WEST only	
Alaska to United States of America	Head SOUTH then EAST	
United States of America to Bahamas	Head SOUTH only	
TOTAL (Nautical Miles Travelled)		

The Bridge

The command centre of the ship, where navigation, speed and the main functions are carried out.

The Bridge was a very old nautical term that originated from the narrow, raised platform joining the two paddle sides of the first paddle wheel steam-powered vessels. Historically, there was a wheel for steering. Today, a ship's navigation bridge consists of either; joysticks, controls, and buttons.

Take the CON

To take over, or control, of the navigational duties on the bridge of the ship.

Answers on page 148

63

FIND A WORD

Find a few words. On the ship, you may have heard.

D	K	P	I	Z	Z	A	B	O	W	A	B
M	I	D	S	H	I	P	T	A	R	C	S
S	D	N	L	H	Z	E	T	F	I	A	T
T	S	H	I	P	O	E	M	T	C	P	A
E	C	M	P	N	R	P	P	A	E	T	R
R	L	F	U	S	G	O	I	N	C	A	B
N	U	R	L	S	O	R	F	C	R	I	O
N	B	I	P	L	T	T	O	H	E	N	A
S	D	Z	Z	C	R	E	W	O	A	G	R
E	B	U	F	F	E	T	R	R	M	U	D

AFT
ANCHOR
BOW
BUFFET
CAPTAIN
CREW
DINING ROOM
FUN
ICE CREAM
KIDS CLUB
MIDSHIP
MUSTER
PIZZA
POOL
PORT
SHIP
SHOP
STARBOARD
STERN
WATERSLIDE

Answers on page 148

Cruising One Port at a time — Cindy's Journal Entry Seven

Dear Journal,

Today, early morning, the ship reached a port day. A lot of passengers were getting ready to go on their way. Mom pointed out that the strength of the sun's rays always goes unseen. She advised me to pack a hat, sunglasses, and sunscreen. I know it is not cool being a red prawn, as that causes skin cancer and can have your life torn.

We walked off the ship and onto the wharf, where the crew directed everyone onto the shore. Dad told me that tomorrow at our next port, the ship is too big for the dock, and we will need to catch a tender boat, leaving less time on the clock.

I observed my father repeatedly checking the time, as our late return to the vessel could have resulted in us being left behind. If you miss the ship, it's no fun getting whipped. If you get caught running along the dock, the only place you would end up is on TikTok!

Docking at the wharf meant we had more time at the beach and exploring the port. There was so much to see and do that I was never bored. I couldn't wait to learn about other people's cultures and ways. I enjoyed their tropical food, and I had my hair done in braids. The best part of visiting islands in remote places, I got to see so many faces.

The water was crystal clear, whilst swimming near the pier. As I snorkelled around, there were many turtles and fish to be found. Swimming and playing in the sand, I looked at mom and dad and was very thankful for the gift they gave me and how much this holiday took to be planned.

I wanted to collect from the beach the shells, flowers, and some sand. But dad said that I had to be mindful that bringing items onto the ship or home may be banned. I left all the items behind, as I didn't want my family to get fined. On embarking; the ship's security scanned our bags. Luckily, I did not keep any banned items, as some had theirs taken and tagged. I am exploring one port at a time; my life is at its prime.

Cruising life; Thanks for today, an adventure full of sunshine rays!

Story continues Page 77

Colour the picture

ESCAPE ROOM #7
Enter if you dare

Unlock Cindy's journal

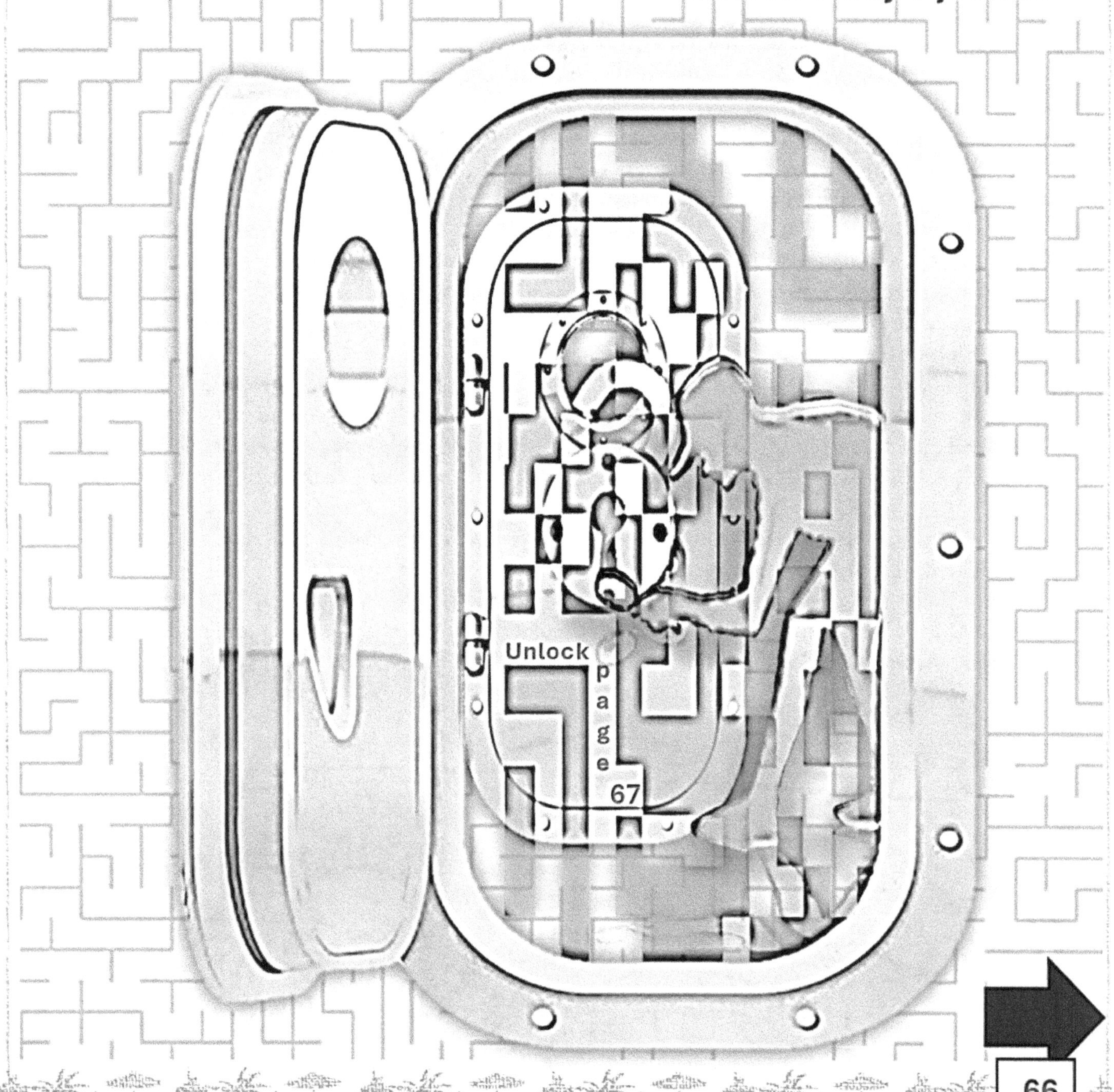

Unlock page 67

66

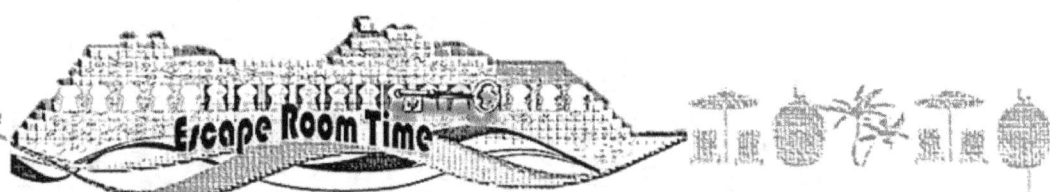

Escape, but don't make a mistake!

Oh no Cindy's journal is locked. You must solve puzzles to get out and through each section of her adventures before the ship docks.

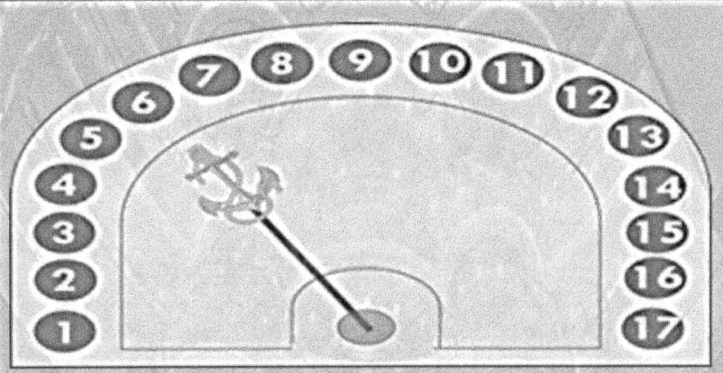

You enter on deck 6; you need to be on 4, but what deck did you get out on, when it finally opened the door.

Catch the lift to 3 decks above you.

Wait the door did not open. It has taken you down 2 decks.

Oops someone jumped in and did not let you out. The lift has now gone down 3 decks.

Oh no! someone pressed too many buttons. The lift has now gone up 2 decks. This is the deck that you get out.

Solve the lift movements to get the next code. Be careful as the lift has a mind of its own. If too many buttons are pressed, it will take you to the unknown. Write the deck you ended up getting out of in the box below.

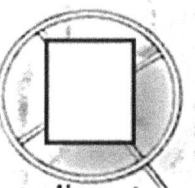

Also, write the code on page 103

Answers on page 148

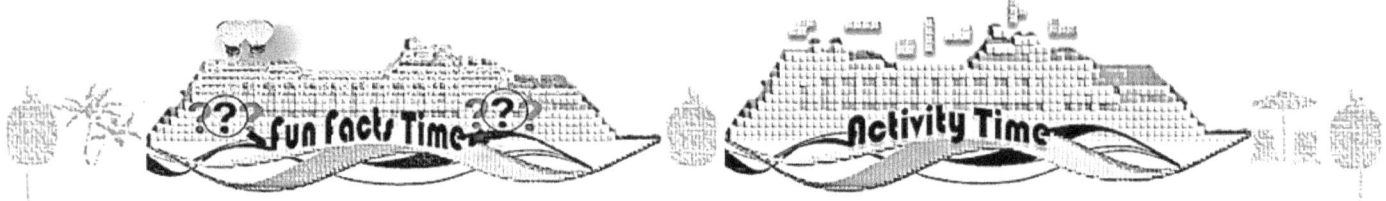

Power up all your energy and have fun
For this is how the ship is run.

Cruise ships use either gas turbines, diesel-electric or diesel engines. The engines are used for propulsion and provide electric power throughout the ship. The most types used by cruise ships are diesel engines. Some of the electricity goes to the propulsion and the rest to the running of the ship. There is also Liquefied Natural Gas (LNG) powered engines. Heat from these engines are used for onboard electricity, and they can plug into electricity supplies at ports when docked.

Did you know that when the ship is docked, they may use the shore power. Also known as; Shore-to-ship. The ships can plug-in to renewable energy from the shore, this allows them to power down their main engines – reducing emissions, noise and air pollution.

Connect the six boxes without crossing any lines. Draw a line connecting the two boxes labelled A. Draw another line connecting the boxes labelled B. Draw a third line connecting the boxes labelled C. The lines cannot touch each other. The lines can't go outside of the box. The lines don't have to be straight; you can curve them. 'B' has been completed for you.

Oops, the ship has stalled, now its time to be an engineer... you have been called. Reconnect the ships power while the generator is on, as you don't want to have a cold shower.

Propulsion is the way ships generate power to move through the water.

Power can be different from ship to ship

Answers on page 149

OH NO!   THE PORT HOLE OPENED UP

COLOUR THE PICTURE BEFORE THE SEA CREATURES RUN A MUCK

Activity Time

Draw a hand crab

Trace your left hand →

Trace your right hand →

Draw an Octopus

Sun-safe Trip

Clothing that covers the arms — S _ _ _ _
Protects your eyes — S _ _ _ _ _ _ _ _ _
Covers your head, face, ears — H _ _
Cover your skin — S _ _ _ _ _ _ _ _
An umbrella provides — S _ _ _ _
The sun can cause this disease — C _ _ _ _ _

Place these items into the crossword below

Don't be a fan of a Tan

It is not too late to start Beauty is found in your heart

When you go to the shore, it is important to have a sun-safe return.

There is one ugly thing that you will need to avoid, even if there are clouds, it will sure still burn.

You will need to pack at least these 5 items for a sun safe day.

But don't worry, these minimum items may help protect you from the sun's burning rays.

Skin is the largest organ of your body

Skin cancer can occur by exposure to the ultraviolet radiation rays from the sun, where it damages skin cells.

Don't be a fan of the tan! The burn may take a turn!
Don't let the sunburn play hide and seek!
Put a shirt and cream on, to help have skin cancer beat!

Answers on page 149

Fun Facts
Cruise Ships in Port

The Pilot

Maritime Pilots are people that have knowledge of harbour waterways. They know local details such as depth, currents, and hazards, and protect the living plants and sea life. They board and and join the ship's crew to safely guide the ship.

Tugboats

Newer Cruise Ships use bow/stern thrusters and pods to move in and out of the port, but sometimes tugboats may still be needed. The wind may have a lot of force, and the Captain may require the tugboats for many other reasons.

Anchors

Cruise ships have between 2 to 4 anchors for different reasons, such as stabilising the ship during bad weather conditions, securing the ship while docked, and for emergency situations. Even though the newer cruise ships rely on their engines for moving, they may still use anchors in the event that the propulsion breaks down.

Also, they may need to keep the ship's position. When the cruise ship does not use a port, then tenders (small boats) are used to get you to the port and the anchors may be used. Cruise ship anchors can weigh anywhere from 10,000kgs to 20,000kgs.

Ropes or Lines?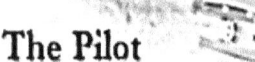

On a ship the ropes are called lines. There are many types of lines, including mooring lines, dock lines, and tow lines. Mooring lines are used for mooring the ship to the dock.

Rats

Have you seen a disk-like object on the ropes? These are rat guards that prevent them from climbing the lines onto the ship during docking at the port.

Colour the Turtle

Learn some fun facts while you get a pencil.
When you are at the beach you may swim near a turtle, so please learn to be gentle.

Sea turtles lay their eggs in a nest they dig in the sand with their rear flippers.

Sea turtles may be one of the oldest creatures on earth.

There are around 7 different species of sea turtles in the world, and they live majority of their lives out at sea.

Sea turtles cannot pull their heads into their shell for safety.

You will cruise one port at a time
So off you go, beat the disembarking line!

Don't forget your hat! The crew and your friends will see you when you get back!

Sunscreen each day steers the cancer away!

Start here

Have a great Port day!

Answers on page 149

74

Activity Time Colouring Time

There are dolphins following the ship at sea

It's a sign of good luck, find them in this picture and write how many there are here.

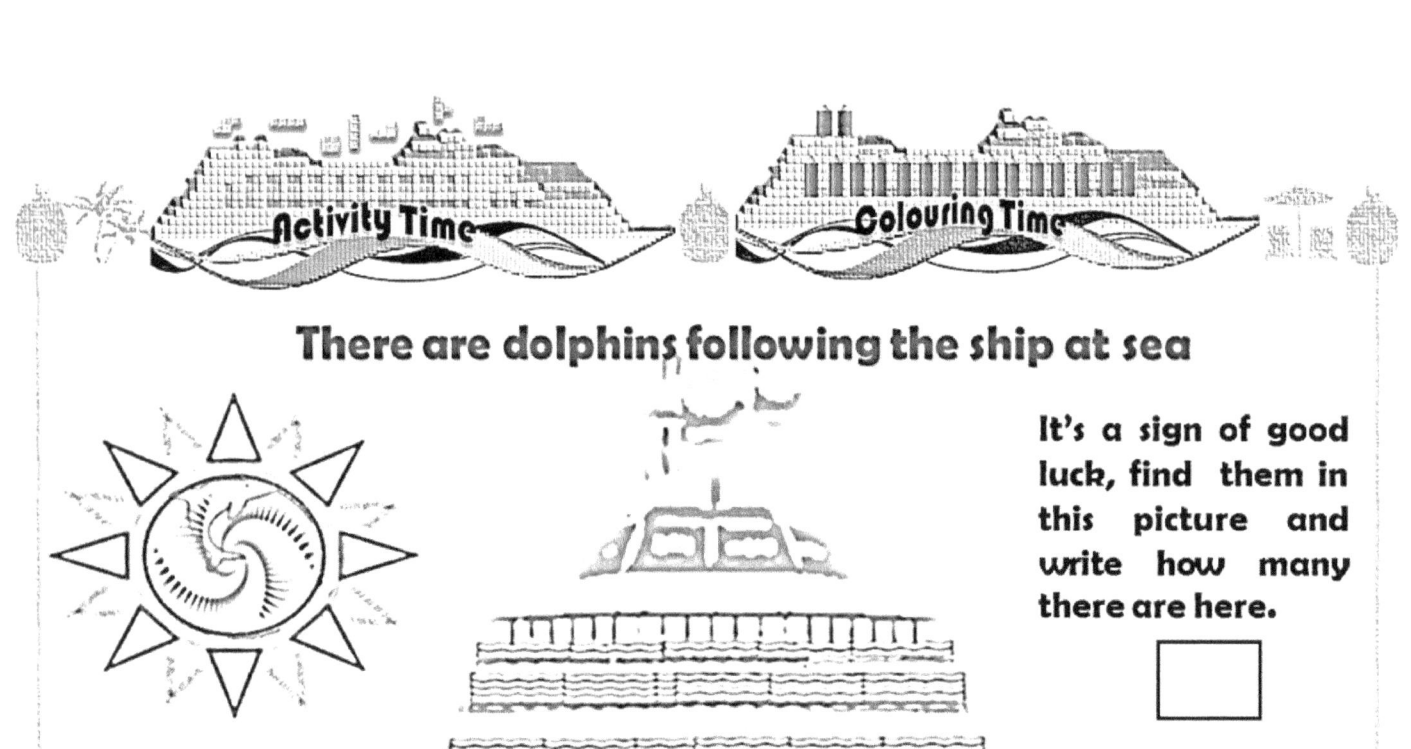

Colour the picture   Answers on page 149

Sea Days & Ways to Play
Cindy's Journal Entry Eight

Dear Journal,

I love the food, and each day the chefs carve a fresh surprise. There is so much to choose from, most days I cannot decide.

Other than food, the activity choice is bountiful, especially the fun games we play in the pool.

Activities, puzzles, trivia, bingo and music are everywhere you turn. Most of all, I love to chill out, read, and watch adults make a fool of themselves, for these are the life lessons we learn.

There are adult areas we cannot visit, but we have enough areas for ourselves, we don't miss it. Watching adults be silly and act differently than they usually do, I wonder how much fun it is also for all the crew.

It is fun being with my new friends as they encourage me to go with them to all the activities, even when I usually hide from all the people and the ongoing festivities.

I have recorded all the things I enjoy, and if it is too much or noisy, I will play in the arcade or with my favourite toy. We had a pirate themed party, yo-ho me hearties! And we got to carry out a walk-the-plank play. Oh, this trip has been full of fun each day!

At the teens club, there have been a few people to meet. I am enjoying this cruise with every heartbeat.

Cruising life; Thank you for today, life is great, what else can I say!

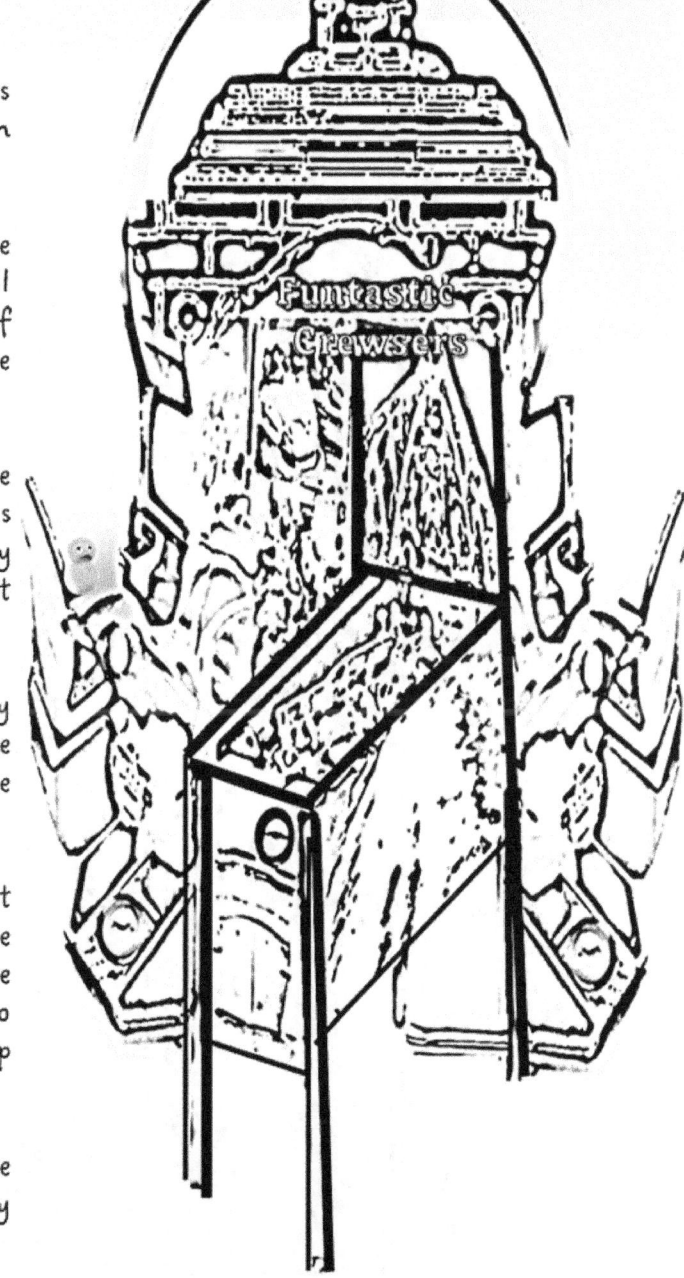

#8

ESCAPE ROOM
Enter if you dare

Unlock Cindy's journal

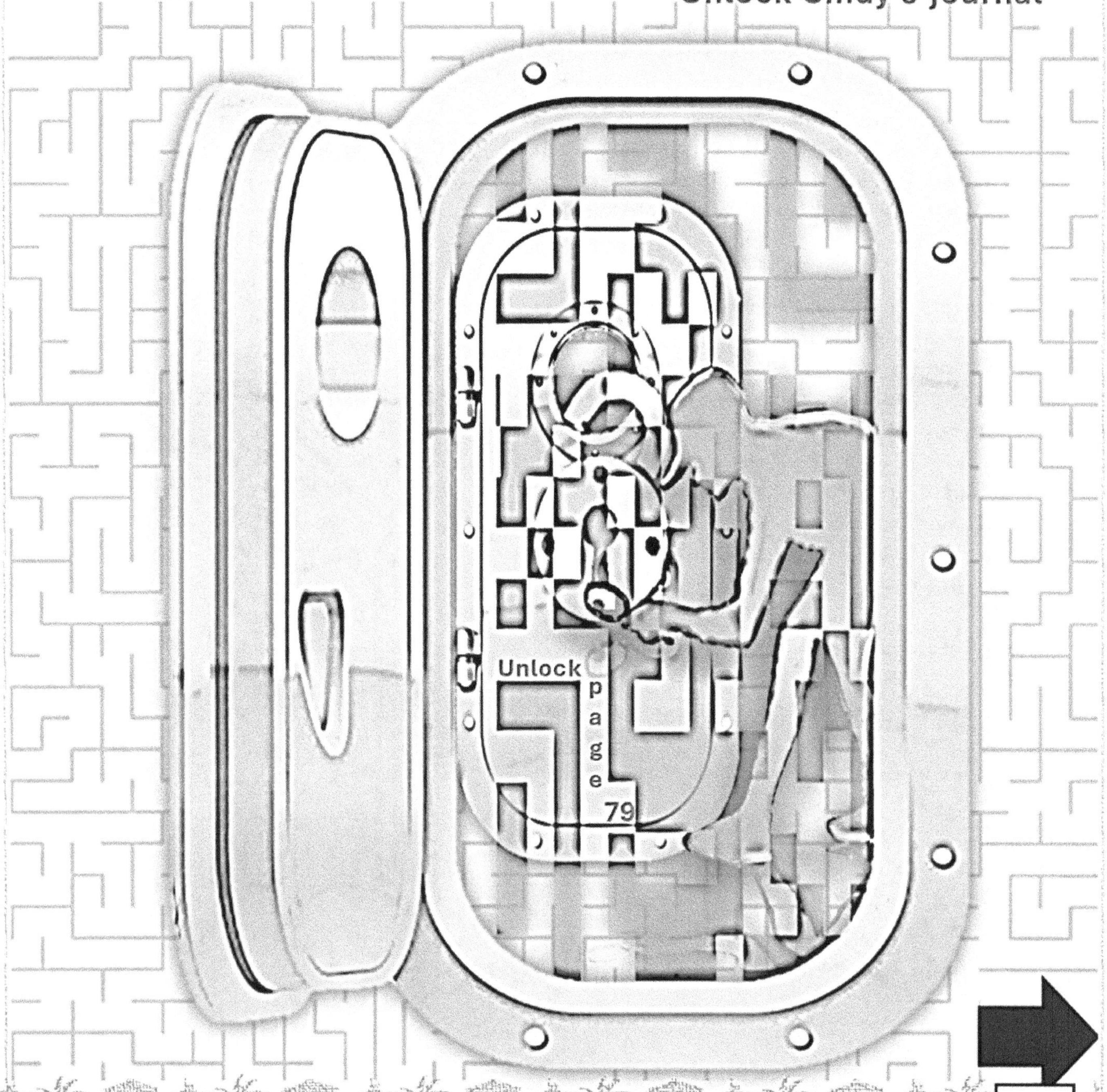

Unlock page 79

78

Escape, but don't make a mistake!

Oh no Cindy's journal is locked. You must solve puzzles to get out and through each section of her adventures before the ship docks.

Holidaying	on a	cruise ship is	a breeze
in the	ocean	Life	is fun when
you learn	and	play at sea.	Because
cruising	the waves	sets	you free!

You would usually sit __ _ chair.

Live _ _ _ _ to your fullest.

School is where _ _ _ _ _ _ _ .

Let the sea set _ _ _ _ _ _ _ !

Solve the sentences by using words from each line of puzzles. Each solved word has a letter that will spell a number. Write the number you decoded and put it in the box below.

Also, write the code on page 103

Answers on page 150

79

6 Pocket - 9 Ball Sudoku!

There are 3 balls that need to be pocketed. There was a call shot for the 3 remaining balls to be rocketed. Find out what those balls are.

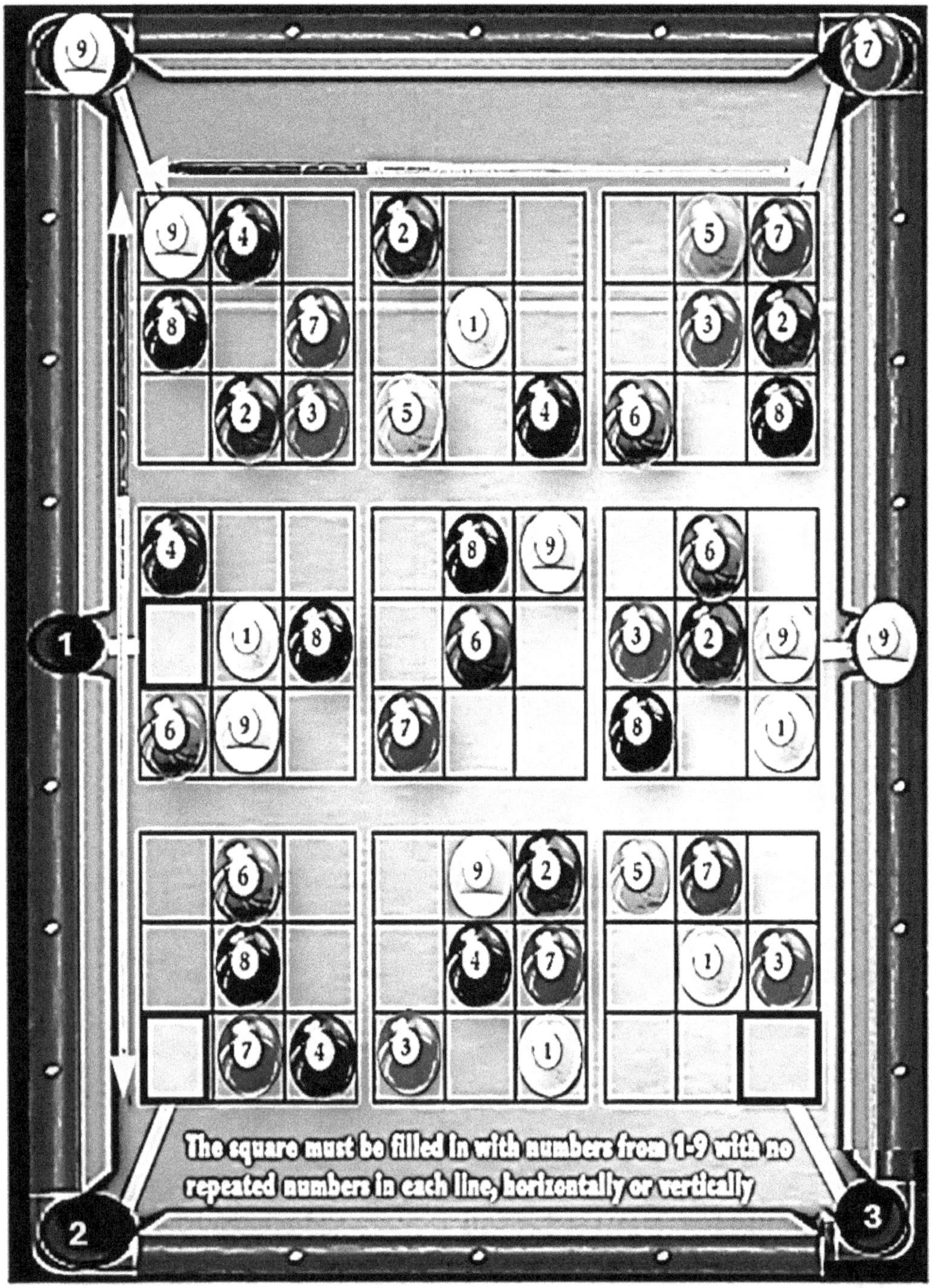

HOW TO PLAY

Each row, column and square (9 spaces within 9 boxes) needs to be filled out with the numbers 1-9, without repeating any numbers within the row, column or square.

FUN FACT
Have you used a Pool Table on a cruise ship?

Have you wondered how you can still play with the sway? The table is automatically adjusted according to the movements calculated by the sensors of the moving ship. This means that the table remains stable. The technical term is a gyroscopic designed pool table.

Answers on page 150

A MUTINY — In the earlier days...

ARRR, ON THE PLANK! WHO HAS TAKEN OVER THE RANK?

Where did we find the cheeky one? What was found at the Helm?

	Buffet	Bridge	Cabin	Pool	Sports area	Cookie	Compass	Headset	Snorkel	Towel Animal
Captain										
Chef										
Cabin Crew										
Cindy										
Squiggly										
Cookie										
Compass										
Headset										
Snorkel										
Towel Animal										

There is a mutiny on the cruise ship. Someone has taken the helm, navigated to Mystery Island, to take a break and catch some fish.

Investigate who did it, and what they left behind. You are the detective that will solve this cheeky crime.

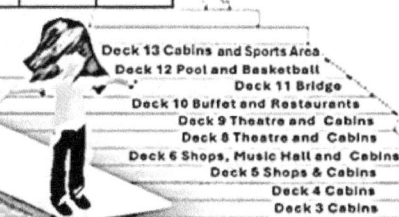

Deck 13 Cabins and Sports Area
Deck 12 Pool and Basketball
Deck 11 Bridge
Deck 10 Buffet and Restaurants
Deck 9 Theatre and Cabins
Deck 8 Theatre and Cabins
Deck 6 Shops, Music Hall and Cabins
Deck 5 Shops & Cabins
Deck 4 Cabins
Deck 3 Cabins
Deck 2 Cabins
Deck 1 Cabins

1. The Chef is in a place that is on deck 10.
2. Squiggly was caught with an item that is used when you are wet, however the crew use this to create fun animals.
3. The Cabin Crew, as well as the one that is in the pool, had an item that starts with the letter 'C'.
4. The Captain is either in the pool or sports area.
5. The one that is in the Cabin, also has the towel animal.
6. Cindy is on deck 12.
7. The one on the bridge had the cookie.
8. Squiggly is asleep on deck 3.
9. The Cabin Crew kept leaving crumbs.
10. The Chef had taken a breathing device.
11. The cheeky one that walks the plank is fishing amongst the rank, on deck 11.

What item was found at the scene of the crime? _____

Who caused the mutiny? taking the helm. _____
Oh! They are the cheeky one!

Answers on page 150

A CRIME ON BOARD — In the present days...

Let's quantum leap from the 17/18th Century to the current day which is the 21st Century.

You won't be forced off the ship by the plank. A mutiny was regarded as a very serious offence (crime), as it caused a major safety concern, because the people were taking over the control of the ship from the Captain. Previously, the power was given to the commanding officer to inflict a death penalty without a need of a court. But now, if you commit a crime at sea, you may end up locked in a brig, normally located in the lower decks. (Brig is derived from brigantine). This is the nautical term for a jail (gaol). There are specialised and trained crew on board to keep you safe, and they police the international laws and ship's policies and regulations. If you break any of these rules that warrant the safety of other passengers, then those crew may detain you in the brig or keep you locked (specialised lock) in your cabin. Depending on the crime, the ship may deal with the situation within their own policies or hand you over to the next call of port's Country jurisdiction.

FUN FACT

Under the Ship there is a great big sea

The ocean provides nearly 50% oxygen to the earth, which includes you and me

Colour the picture

Hidden below the sea
Where could the 8 items that fell overboard be?

Find and circle the lost items.......

Cruising Duck   Golf Ball   Hat   Cell phone   Passport   Snorkel set   Sun chair   Sunglasses   Titanic

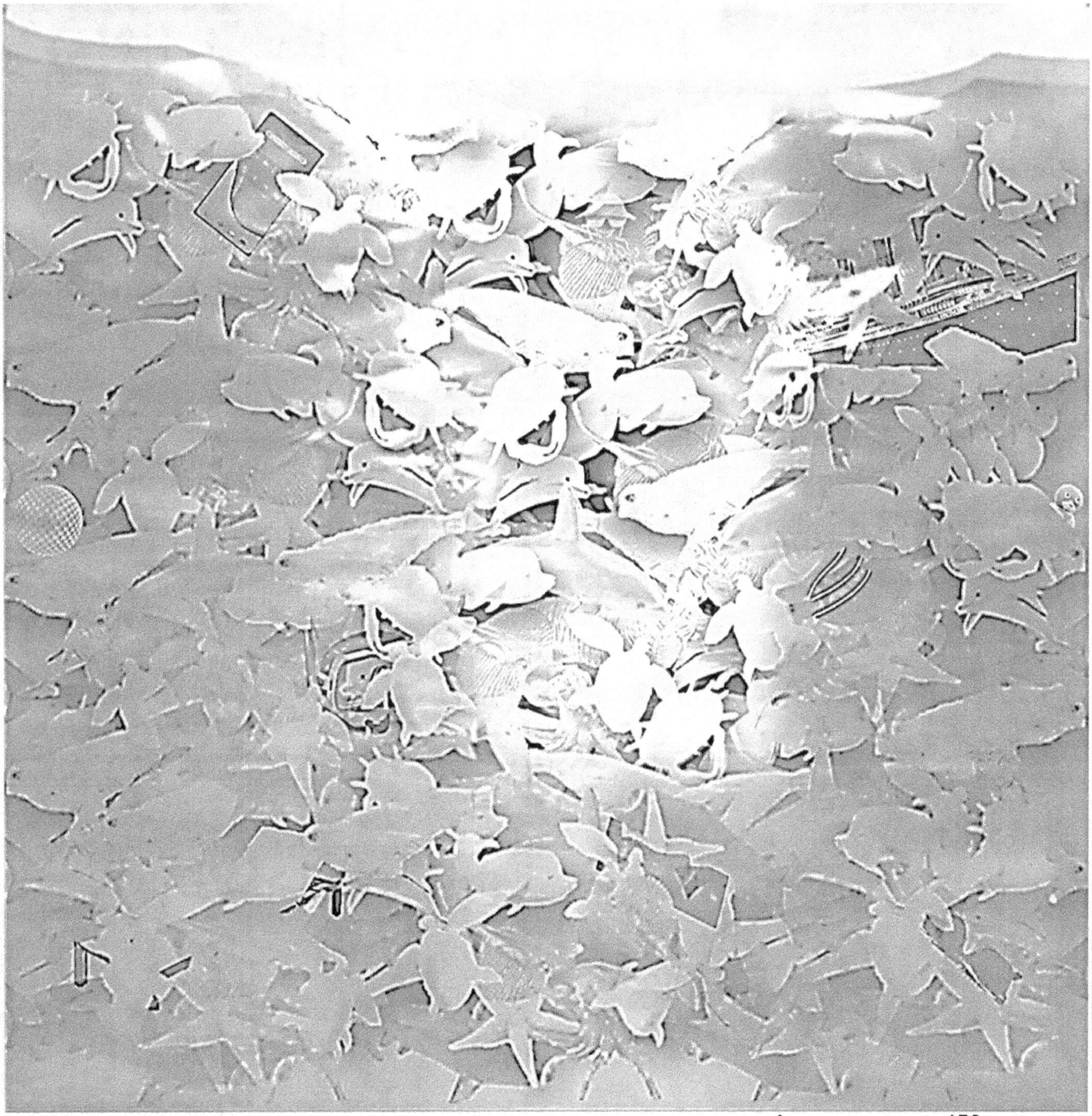

Answers on page 150

Art of the High Seas

The art auction was midway, on midship, and during a mid-wave.
All the paintings have lost their colours.
Can you help repaint with your artistic powers?

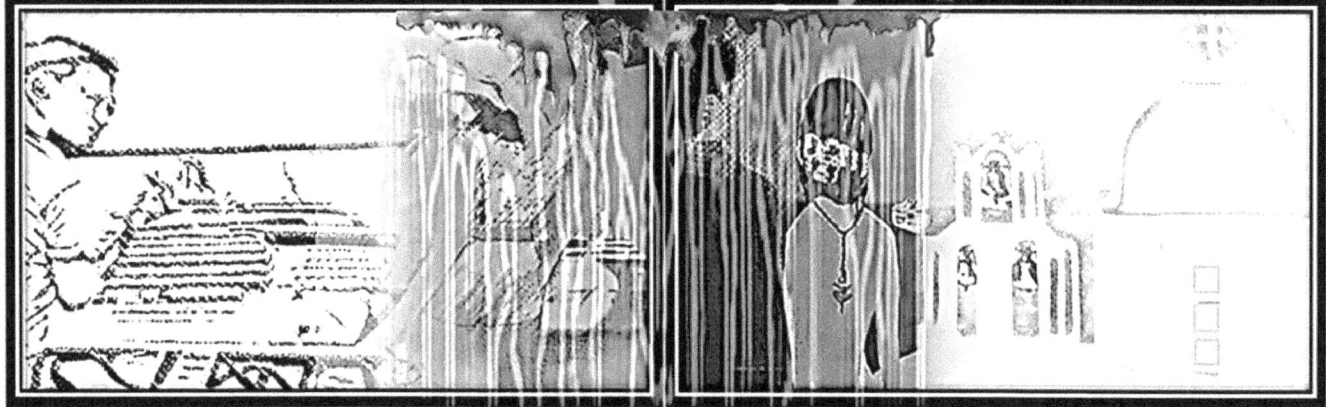

 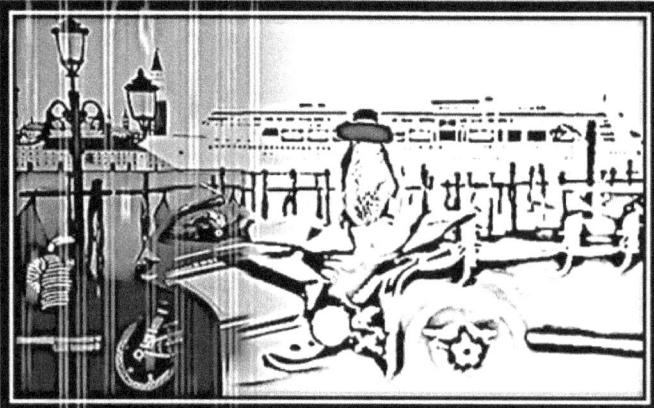

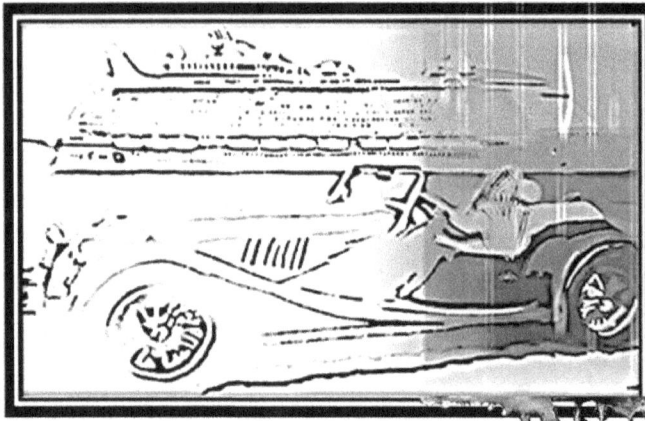 

Colour the pictures

Fun Adventures on the Hunt Cindy's Journal Entry Nine

Dear Journal,

Had a load of fun on the scavenger hunt today. I tried to find what deck things were on and if there were any ducks that were hidden away. It was exciting at every turn; lucky I had a lot of energy to burn.

I was exploring; searching and going through all the sections, passing adults playing; trivia, games, and bingo, where they all seemed to show competitive intentions. I was glad that I had the teen activity tasks ahead, that allowed me to laugh, play, and have fun instead.

We had seen kids running around and pressing all the lift buttons, which were not allowed. They were creating their own fun and upsetting most of the older crowd. As I passed the trivia section, mum pulled me aside, telling me that everyone, no matter what age, is having a holiday. Outside of the teens club, we are with our parents, I always respect the rules and follow the ship's way.

Jacqui, my friend, joked that by doing the right thing, it didn't make us nerds, it just made the rowdy button pressers look like a pack of turds. I think that made me laugh more than the hunt we had to play; it was funny in every way.

I think my imagination always goes wild, but at the same time I know that by doing the right thing, there will be no-one judging or forcing me to be anything other than a child.

I like how cruising fun facts, games, and adventures are not like the farm or school. This holiday is a time for me to let go, do something different, and act very cool.

Cruising life; Thanks for today, mom and dad's gift holiday!

ESCAPE ROOM #9
Enter if you dare

Unlock Cindy's journal

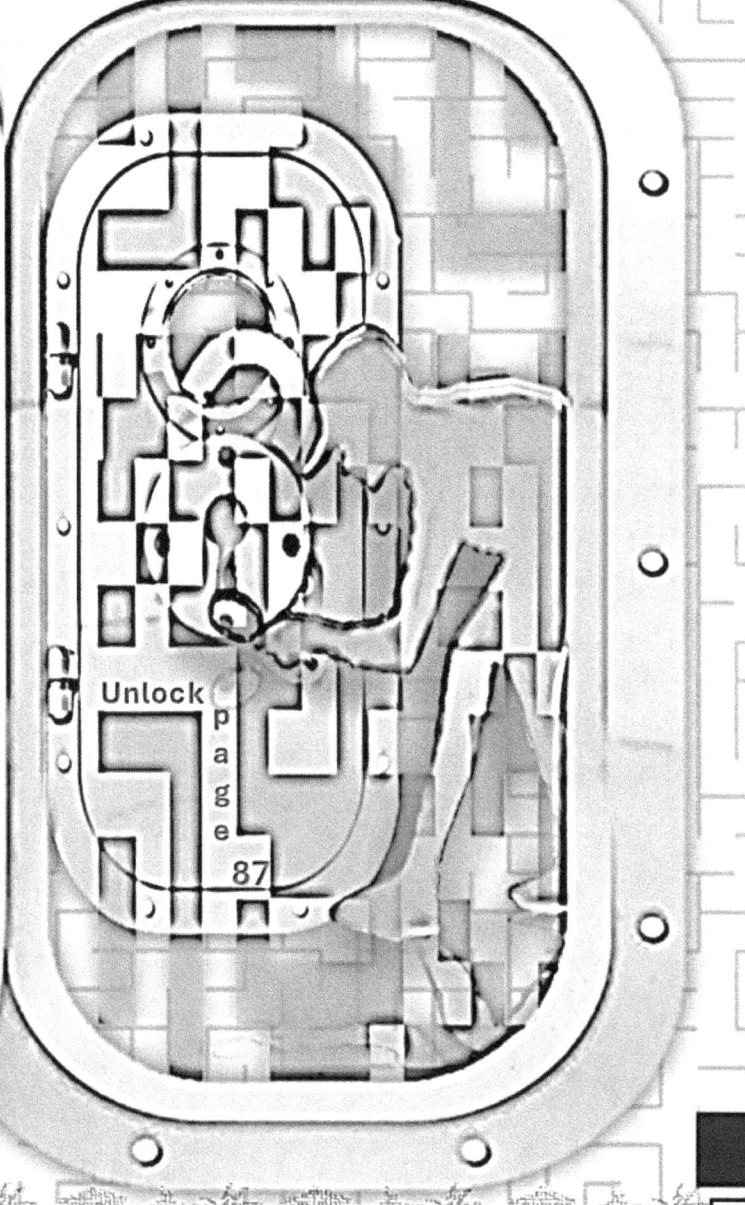

Unlock page 87

86

Escape, but don't make a mistake!

Oh no Cindy's journal is locked. You must solve puzzles to get out and through each section of her adventures before the ship docks.

Enter Passcode

Speaker system sounds:
1. ••• • •••— • —•
2. ••• •• •———
3. — •••• — ———
4. — ••— —••

You have had too much fun around the ship. You turn to your phone and notice it has locked. You have forgotten the code. But don't worry, there is a sound on the speaker system. Carefully listen or you may miss a beat. Write the codes in the white boxes. Now write the number that is in section number 2 (ship), into the box below.

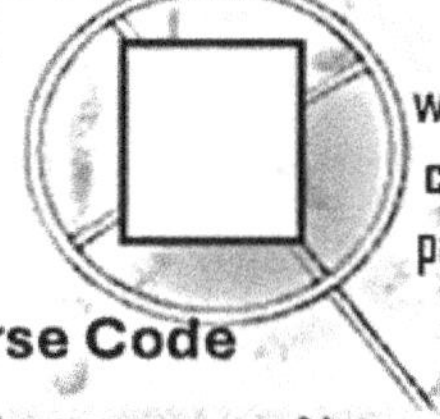

Also, write the code on page 103

Morse Code

Answers on page 151

87

FUN FACTS
OLD SAILOR SUPERSTITIONS & CRUISE SHIPS

Ships have a coin tradition that dates to Roman times, where coins were attached to a ship to provide protection. Ask the staff where the ship coin is located. Some cruise ships have it located on the radar mast.

If dolphins follow the ship, it's a sign of good luck.

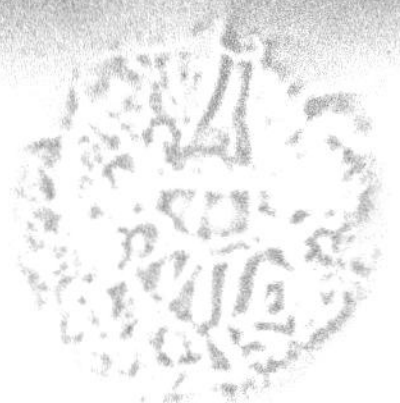

Since the 20th century cruise ships have a godmother for good luck, by smashing of a bottle across a new ship's hull. In ancient times wine was used where men spilled the wine on purpose to check for cracks in the hull

A sail-away party where adults are toasting with champagne to have a good time, may give them good luck for a Bon Voyage.

Step on the ship with your right foot, it may be bad luck to step onboard a ship with your left foot first.

Don't whistle whilst on the Bridge, because you might whistle up a storm.

Seaward Hunt

Even if you lose your way,
you will always find these items, whilst you enjoy your stay

Tick and/or take photos

- ✖ Life raft [Deck]
- ✖ Lifesaver [Deck]
- ✖ Anchor [Deck]
- ✖ Piano [Deck]
- ✖ Library/Games [Deck]
- ✖ Shops [Deck]
- ✖ Kids Pool [Deck]
- ✖ Decorations on a stateroom door [Deck]
- ✖ Cruise Duck/Live bird [Deck]
- ✖ Your Kids Club [Deck]
- ✖ Pizza/Hotdogs [Deck]
- ✖ Life Jacket [Deck]
- ✖ Buffet [Deck]
- ✖ Your Muster station [Deck]
- ✖ The ship's Bridge [Deck]
- ✖ Bingo [Deck]
- ✖ Theatre [Deck]
- ✖ Ice-cream [Deck]
- ✖ Information [Deck]
- ✖ Your Cabin [Deck]
- ✖ port hole [Deck]
- ✖ Basketball [Deck]

Who am I?
Find out who is at the Helm! Make sure the riddles don't make you feel overwhelmed!

Hint: The highest grade of licensed seafarer qualification at sea.

Answers on page 151

Who am I?

Riddle me, Riddle me not! Can you see the answer on the spot!

I guide you to your destination, pointing you to your vacation. Without me, you may steer astray, relying on me night and day. Who am I? _ _ T _ _ _ _ _

I sail the high seas, but my ship relies on the breeze. I board other vessels without a ticket. I seek treasure but I'm not rich or give you an enjoyable adventure. Who am I? _ _ I _ _ _ _

I have a deck but not a card, I master the sea, where dolphins are my guard, I may dwell, but most think I am swell. Who am I? _ _ _ _ I _ _ _ _ _

I stand tall and bright; you will see me mainly at night. You use me so you don't hit the shore, but others like to climb me during their tour. Who am I? _ _ _ _ T _ _ _ _ _

I travel the world but have no passport. I have your belongings but never use them. I am always with you when we travel, but I am not your friend. Who am I? _ _ _ _ A _ _ _

I am everywhere for you to see, hanging around not wanting to be used, but you need me. An emergency may happen one day where you throw me away, but you must bring me back in. Who am I? _ _ _ _ N _ _ _

I have both oceans and seas but no water, nor people but I have countries, cities and borders. I am on demand and at your command. Who am I? _ _ _ _ _ _ _ _ _ _ I _ _ _

I cater for a mob, but I am not in that job. I let people walk all over me, but I am stronger than you see. I keep you safe whilst you embark and disembark. Who am I? _ _ _ N _ _ _ _ _

When you need me, you throw me away, but you always take me back. I keep you from going adrift where the sea may pull. Who am I? _ _ _ H _ _

I was known to be unsinkable, but in legends of icebergs, my memory lies. A tragic maiden voyage, under cold skies, I am taboo on ships, never to be described. Who am I? _ _ T _ _ _ _ _

I cover most of the world, where my tops are sometimes curled, I dip deeper than you can go, with sunken ship secrets and myths flow. Who am I? _ _ _ _ C _

I keep you on course, navigate, and set cruise control. I used to be a lonely wheel that you manually turned, but now, I am part of bigger things, that automatically returns. Who am I? _ _ _ _ O _ _

Cars cross me on land, but here you can only walk and use me to stand. I command and conquer and cannot go unmanned. Who am I? _ _ _ I _ _ _

One letter from each answer will spell out who is at the Helm. **WHO AM I?** _ _ _ _ _ _ _ _ _ _ _ _ _ _

Answers on page 151

91

Quack, Quack, Quack
A farm fun fact! This is what some cruise people may pack!

On Cindy's farm she has ducks named the Campbell's. Her ducks provide them with eggs, and every day they lay, they are cruising in their pond and have no interest in flying away.

On some cruise ships, people hide toy ducks for you to find.

Find out if there are any on your cruise ship, as some may also leave them behind.

Don't be sad if your cruise has no ducks, as some have been hidden in this book, so you can still try your luck.

Beak and Seek write the pages where the ducks are. There are ⓖ⓪ ducks to find in this whole book. *Hint check from beginning to the end

Record the page number and the number of ducks on that page
Include this page. Only count the yellow ducks. Do not count the ducks on any of the answer pages 141-153.

Page #	Ducks	Page #	Ducks	Page #	Ducks	Page #	Ducks	Page #	Ducks

TOTAL DUCKS
# of Pages Ducks

Answers on page 151

Some 'Sea'rious Vacay'ing Cindy's Journal Entry Ten

Dear Journal,

On the ship, mom and dad have limited the Wi-Fi, I thought without technology I was going to die. But with the ship and all the many features, I discover a whole new life full of adventures and watching the sea creatures.

I find joy in my time on board, taking a break from life's responsibilities and chores. At home I complete every job, spend a lot of time on social media and going to school or taking a jog. The cruise ship gives me another part of life I have never experienced before; anything beats having to complete my school homework chores.

A lot of my fun is pretending to be stuck behind the cabin doors, using my imagination to escape through the ship's floors. Cruising is not only for adults, as us children are part of the next generational voyaging life, we are truly intruding into the cruising cult.

I like to pretend to be a crew member for the day, having confidence in knowing my way. Whenever the ship goes into the port, I notice that the flags are out on the top decks signalling the shore. I have fun working out what the flags represent, as it is a great place to explore.

Some people like to muck around or just relax on the deck chairs at the pool. It does not mean that anyone is better or cooler than those that thrive to create an imagination tool. Both adults and children can all enjoy the cruise holiday, feeling like a queen or a star, for life is about everyone being proud of who they really are.

Cruising life; Thank you for today, appreciating my individual way!

Story continues Page 101

Colour the picture

ESCAPE ROOM #10
Enter if you dare
Unlock Cindy's journal

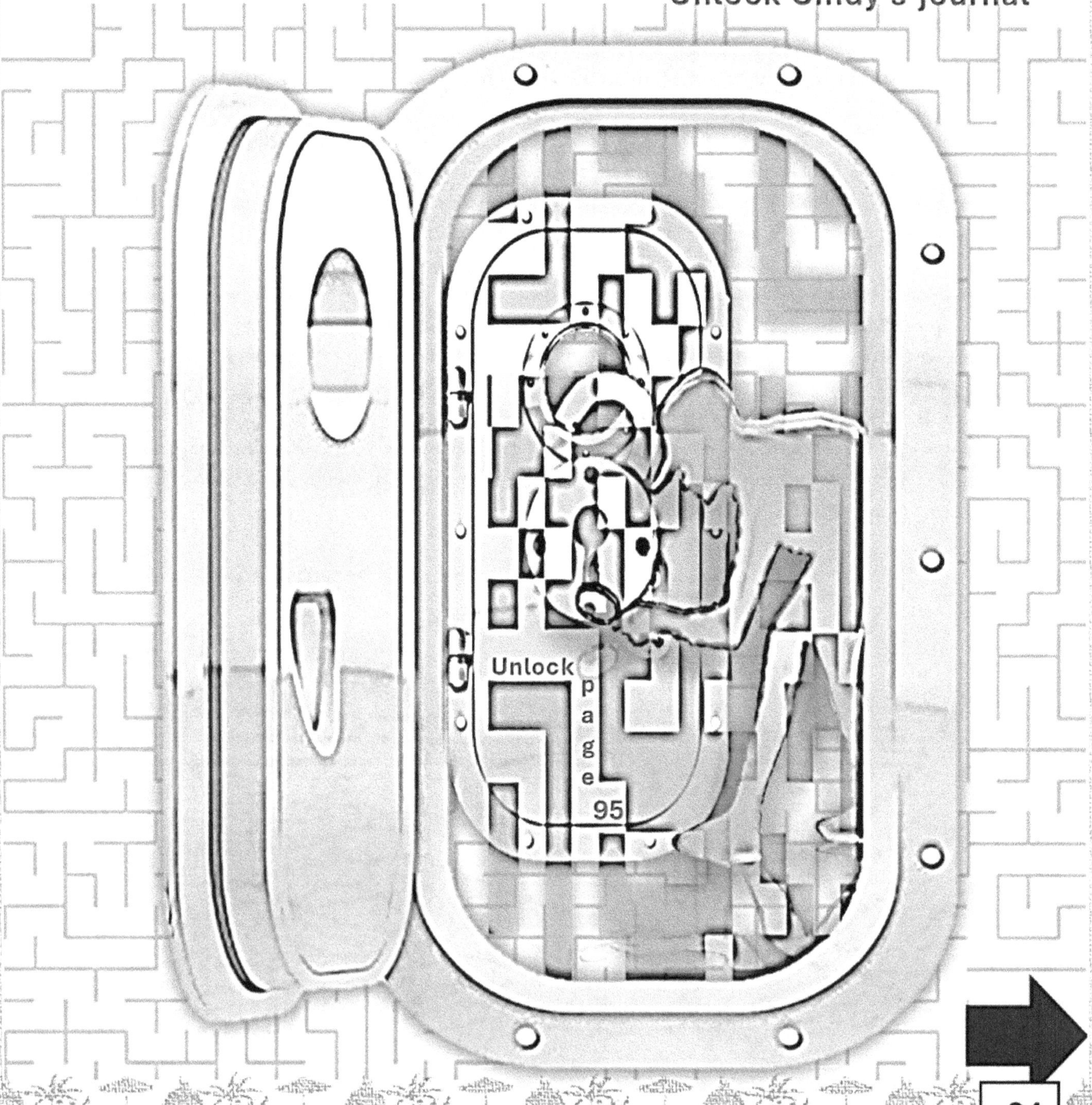

Unlock page 95

International code of signals will break you out!

Wait whilst we turnabout. All the flags fell from the roof. Follow them to become the champion sleuth.

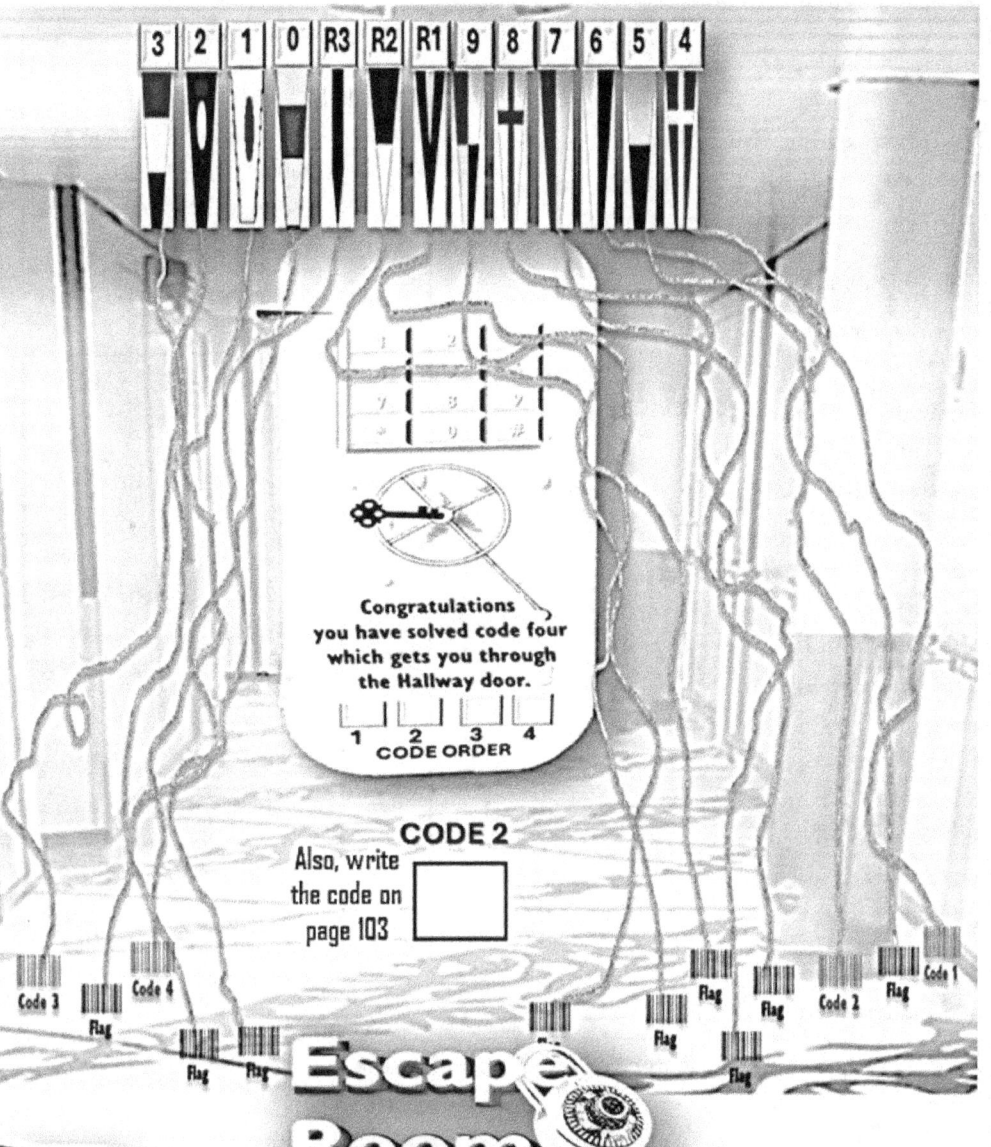

Follow the flag lines, in order, to get the hallway code.

You have managed to escape 9 rooms, but now you will need to make it through the hallway, or you may be doomed.

Dinner time is almost here, so hurry and solve the final code to be in the clear.

Make sure codes 1, 2, 3 and 4 match the flags. As this will help you through to the last stage.

A new code for the hallway will be your code out of the four. The code number 2 will unlock the flags and allow you to gain your hallway pass to enter another door.

SHIP FLAG FUN FACT:
There are 26 nautical flags, each being for a different letter of the alphabet. Each are the international code word connected to the letters of the phonetic alphabet, used by vessels. There are also 10 flags for the numbers zero through to nine. For the numbers 10 and larger, a ship combines the flags.

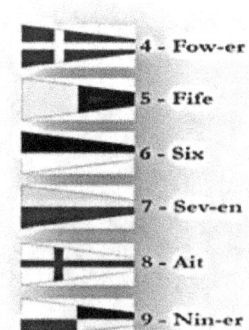

- Repeater 1
- Repeater 2
- Repeater 3
- 0 - Zero
- 1 - Wun
- 2 - Too
- 3 - Tree
- 4 - Fow-er
- 5 - Fife
- 6 - Six
- 7 - Sev-en
- 8 - Ait
- 9 - Nin-er

Answers on page 152

Fun Flag Facts

Don't squawk ……. talk the talk. Be a shipmate and communicate!

- A Alpha (Divers Down)
- B Bravo (I am taking in or discharging or carrying dangerous goods)
- C Charlie (Affirmative/Yes)
- D Delta (Keep clear, I am manoeuvring with difficulty)
- E Echo (Altering course to starboard)
- F Foxtrot (I am disabled, please communicate)
- G Golf (I require a Pilot)
- H Hotel (I have a Pilot on board)
- I India (I am altering course to port)
- J Juliet (I am on fire and have dangerous cargo aboard; keep well clear)
- K Kilo (I wish to communicate with you)
- L Lima (You should stop your vessel instantly)
- M Mike (My vessel is stopped and making no way through the water)
- N November (No/Negative)
- O Oscar (Man Overboard)
- P Papa (All aboard, vessel is about to proceed to sea)
- Q Quebec (My vessel is healthy, and I request free pratique)
- R Romeo (I have received your signal)
- S Sierra (My engines are going full speed astern)
- T Tango (Keep clear of me, I am engaged in pair trawling)
- U Uniform (You are running into danger)
- V Victor (Require assistance – not in distress)
- W Whiskey (I require medical assistance)
- X X-ray (Stop carrying out your intentions and watch for my signals)
- Y Yankee (I am dragging my anchor)
- Z Zulu (I require a tug)

Cruise ships will fly the flag of the country they are visiting as a sign of respect. The port state flag may be flown from the mainmast.

There are 26 nautical flags, each being for a different letter of the alphabet.

Each are the international code word connected to the letters of the phonetic alphabet, used by vessels.

There are also 10 international flags for the numbers zero through to nine. For the numbers 10 and larger, a ship combines the flags.

Phonetic Alphabet

A – Alpha	N – November
B – Bravo	O – Oscar
C – Charlie	P – Papa
D – Delta	Q – Quebec
E – Echo	R – Romeo
F – Foxtrot	S – Sierra
G – Golf	T – Tango
H – Hotel	U – Uniform
I – India	V – Victor
J – Juliet	W – Whiskey
K – Kilo	X – X-Ray
L – Lima	Y – Yankee
M – Mike	Z – Zulu

Ships may fly one flag or up to seven flags in a row. Some flags are read together.

❖ The combination of the D (Delta) and V (Victor) flags, means "I'm manoeuvring with difficulty and require assistance."

❖ The J (Juliet) and L (Lima) flags mean "you're running the risk of going aground."

Most of the time two nautical flags may mean a distress or manoeuvring issue. Three or more flags can include pendants (numbers) and may relate to points of the compass, geographical signals, names of ships, time and position, as well as latitude and longitude.

Signal your name on the ship

You're coming into Port, become one of the Crew. Signal your ship, try something new.

Colour your name by using the Phonetic Alphabet signal flag Colours. Use these flags on the ship to draw and Colour. Use the flags on page 96.

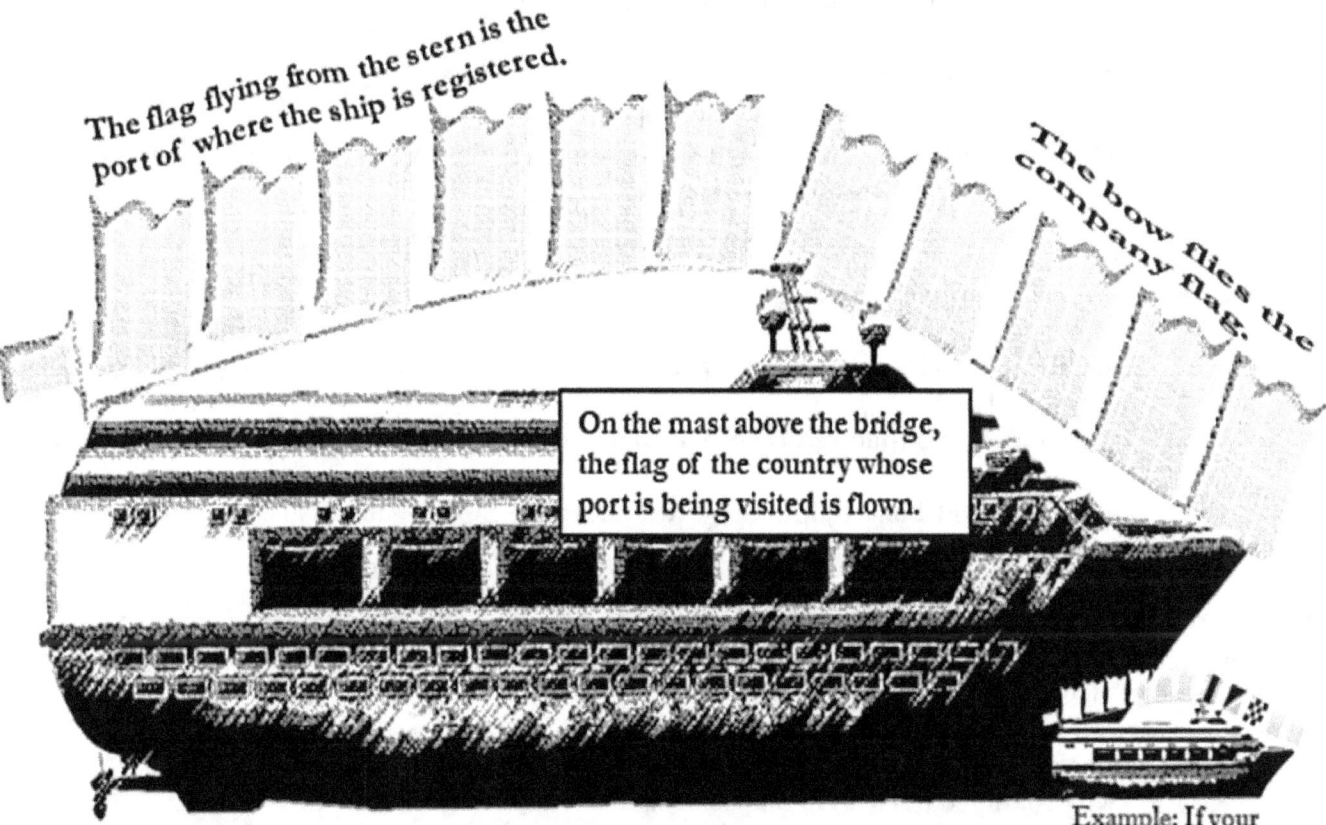

The flag flying from the stern is the port of where the ship is registered.

The bow flies the company flag.

On the mast above the bridge, the flag of the country whose port is being visited is flown.

Ensigns (flags) are commonly flown when entering and leaving the harbour, when sailing through foreign waters, and when the ship is signalled to do so.

Example: If your name was Don

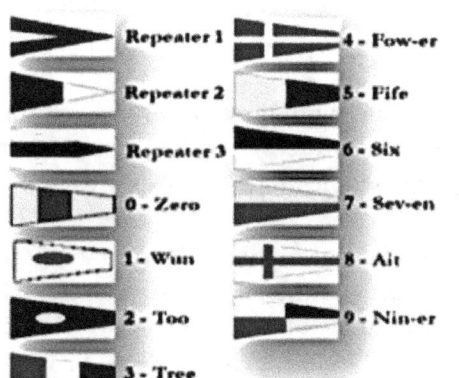

Repeater 1
Repeater 2
Repeater 3
0 - Zero
1 - Wun
2 - Too
3 - Tree
4 - Fow-er
5 - Fife
6 - Six
7 - Sev-en
8 - Ait
9 - Nin-er

Example: 13 years old

Colour your age using the flags

97

The ship's horn will save you in a storm!

Have you ever heard the ship's horn? The sounds are mainly signals to indicate their existence and direction and to avoid collisions at sea, however there are also instances in port and other times the sounds are used to communicate. Here are just three (of many) of the most common instances when the ship's horn may blast.

Manoeuvring signals
If the ship intends to turn, stop, or change speed, the horn may signal:

One short blast: The ship is altering its course to starboard

Two short blasts: The ship is altering its course to port.

Three short blasts: The ship is operating astern propulsion (propelling mechanism is used to develop thrust in a backward direction).

Safe Passing Signals
If the ship is passing another vessel it may signal:

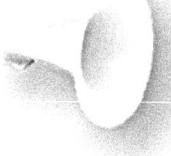

One short blast followed by one prolonged blast: The ship is overtaking another vessel on its starboard side.

Two short blasts followed by one prolonged blast: The ship is overtaking another vessel on its port side.

One prolonged blast followed by two short blasts: The ship is not sure about the other vessel's plans.

Warning Signals
This ship is warning other ships of its existence in the area. These signals are to avoid a collision, and one example is when there is heavy fog:

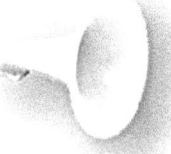

One prolonged blast: The ship is proceeding and is approaching another vessel.

Two prolonged blasts: The ship is being hauled.

Three prolonged blasts: The ship is not under command and cannot or has restricted movement.

You may be asleep, reading a book, or seeking that peace at last. You won't just hear a beep, you may be disturbed and run to have a look, as you will hear a loud blast.

It is not that the Captain is signalling for fun, where it is unfounded. They are under strict regulations of when the signals are to be sounded. It is the price of saving your life! It is essential to sound the appropriate signals to indicate the vessel's presence and direction and avoid collisions.

Vessels are governed by the International Maritime Organization (IMO). Because there are many languages spoken worldwide by mariners, the signals are standardised, where the sound can be recognised by all. The International Rules followed by mariners are called COLREGS. These rules include that vessels must proceed at a safe speed, considering; visibility, traffic density, and the vessel's manoeuvrability.

Are you ready to blow your own horn!
Because there is a high chance of fog increasing from dawn!

Let's play Marco.....Polo! The pool game, originated in America. Swimmers navigate the pool, relying solely on sound to locate and catch the other swimmers playing the game, if the person calling Polo is caught by Marco, then they are next to seek and find. There are many stories on how the game got its name. One indicates that the name Marco Polo comes from the 13th-century Italian trader and explorer Marco Polo. The legend is that 'Marco didn't have a clue as to where he was going'. Another legend is that 'sailors had to communicate on the ships when it was foggy, and they had to use their voices to listen for responses'.

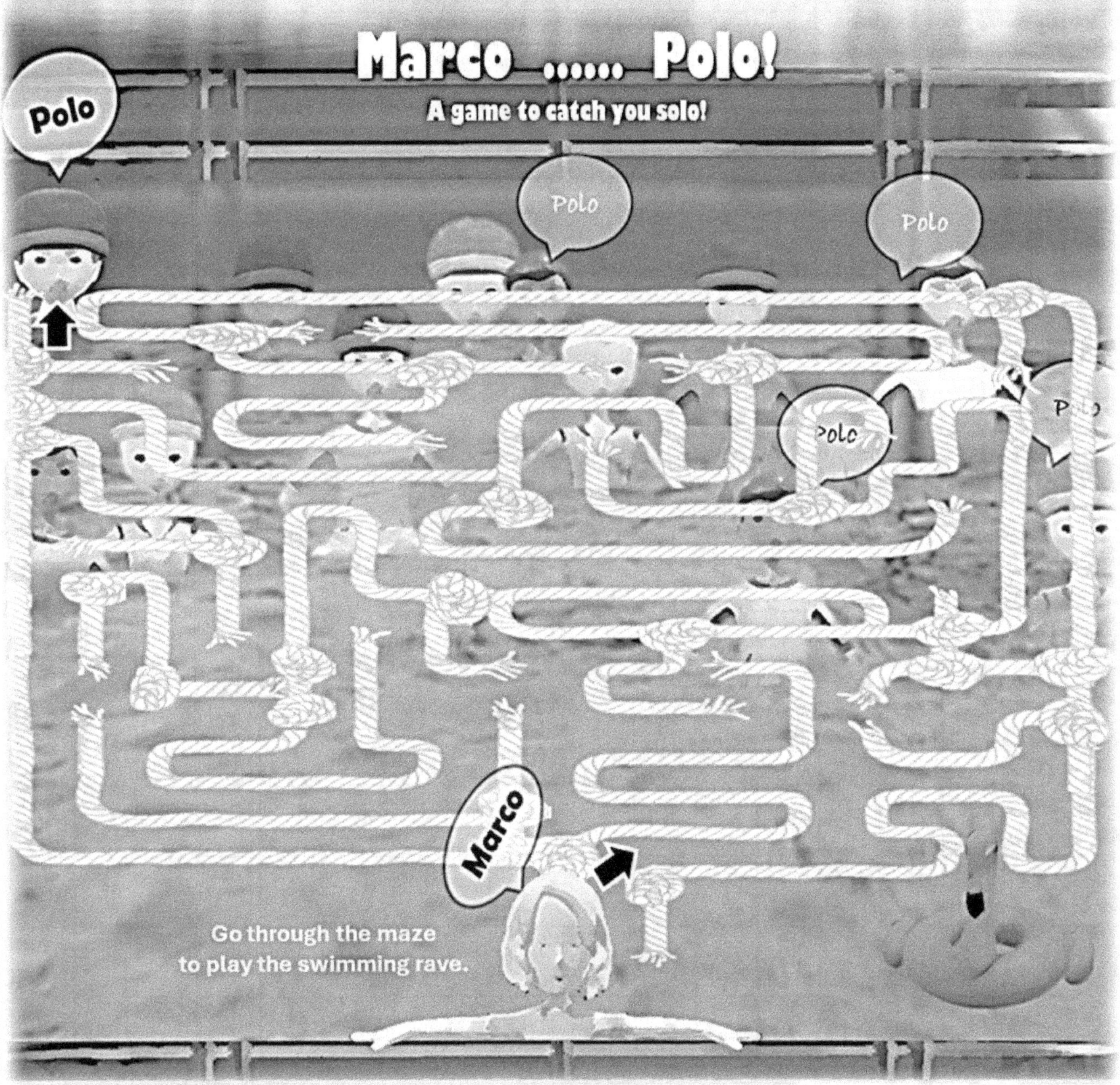

Marco ...... Polo!
A game to catch you solo!

Go through the maze to play the swimming rave.

Answers on page 152

FIND A WORD

The Phonetic Alphabet has been jumbled; help find the words before the flags are tumbled.

I	A	Q	U	E	B	E	C	R	U	I	S	E	R	R	N	O	D
S	N	Z	I	S	E	Y	C	H	A	R	L	I	E	G	O	L	F
A	W	D	N	K	A	L	F	H	O	T	E	L	E	A	V	E	S
I	H	E	I	M	B	R	A	V	O	X	G	W	U	S	E	D	H
L	I	M	A	A									N	K	M	E	E
A	S	Z	L	P									I	F	B	L	L
W	K	I	L	O									F	O	E	T	L
A	E	B	E	S									O	X	R	A	C
Y	Y	P	N	C									R	P	B	N	T
G	R	A	H	A									M	O	W	C	A
V	D	P	N	R									T	Q	M	J	N
I	N	A	O	K									S	P	Y	E	G
C	B	R	Z	A	E	X	S	E	I	F	O	X	T	R	O	T	O
T	K	J	U	L	I	E	T	Z	C	U	I	R	A	D	I	O	T
O	F	F	L	O	N	S	H	I	P	H	E	A	L	P	H	A	B
R	E	D	U	W	S	I	E	R	R	A	O	Y	E	S	I	K	M

Phonetic Alphabet

ALPHA — NOVEMBER
BRAVO — OSCAR
CHARLIE — PAPA
DELTA — QUEBEC
ECHO — ROMEO
FOXTROT — SIERRA
GOLF — TANGO
HOTEL — UNIFORM
INDIA — VICTOR
JULIET — WHISKEY
KILO — XRAY
LIMA — YANKEE
MIKE — ZULU

Answers on page 152

Waving goodbye **Cindy's Journal the end ....**

Dear Journal,

The ship was heading home, and everyone was packing their luggage. It is a different atmosphere, as we were all feeling so sluggish.

While packing, we looked under the beds, cupboards and everywhere. We made sure that all our shoes and socks had their pairs.

I went around and said goodbye to my friends, both old or new. I remembered to exchange details with my future cruising crew.

To get off the ship, we had to scan our card one last time and say goodbye to all the crew. Even though I cannot wait to see Daisy and my farm, it is hard to regain the reality view.

It was sad on the last day to disembark. Looking back at the ship from where the shuttle was parked.

The memories will stay forever. Our cruise time as a family has been filled with love, memories of being together.

I have seized every moment of my cruise holiday. The memories I made as a cruiseling, will pave the future cruising way.

At home I will have to remember that my cruise card won't work, I don't think mom or dad will appreciate waiting on hand and foot, it was truly a cruising perk!

I will remember, for any of my future cruises to; 'seas each and every day. As the cruise ends so fast, as if it was yesterday!

Cruising life; Thank you for today, goodbye such a great vacay!

Colour the picture

The end

Don't risk it for the biscuit!

It is important not to risk entering a country with items that are banned.
As your actions may threaten the health and environment of plants, humans, and animals on or the surrounding that land.

Biosecurity (quarantine)
Government has policies implemented to manage the risks of harmful items entering the country.

Fresh, dried, fruit and vegetables | Meat, Fist, Poultry | Cooking, dairy, poultry bee products | Plants, medicines, animal products | Wood, carvings, straw, feathers, bone | Outdoor gear, dirt, flowers, seeds

Only examples, this is not the full list, each Country has its own regulations.

Declare

Seek advice before you pack, if in doubt put it back!

Always check with the ship's crew and the country that you enter on what is banned or required to be declared!
It is always safer to declare as you are responsible to be aware!

Sam the Biosecurity watch dog has found **6** items in the bag that should have been declared and may be banned.
Can you see them?
Circle the items.

Answers on page 152

102

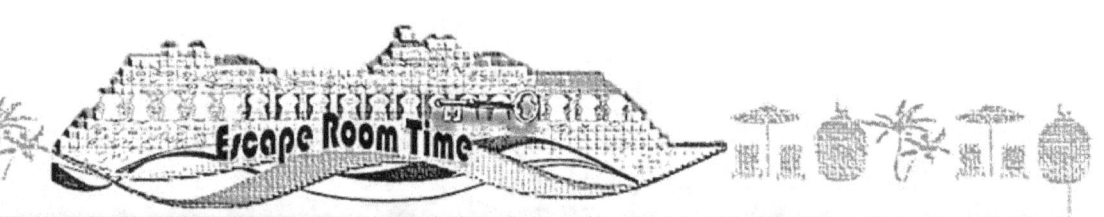

Escape Room Codes!

Oh no Cindy's journal is locked. You must solve puzzles to get out and through each section of her adventures before the ship docks.

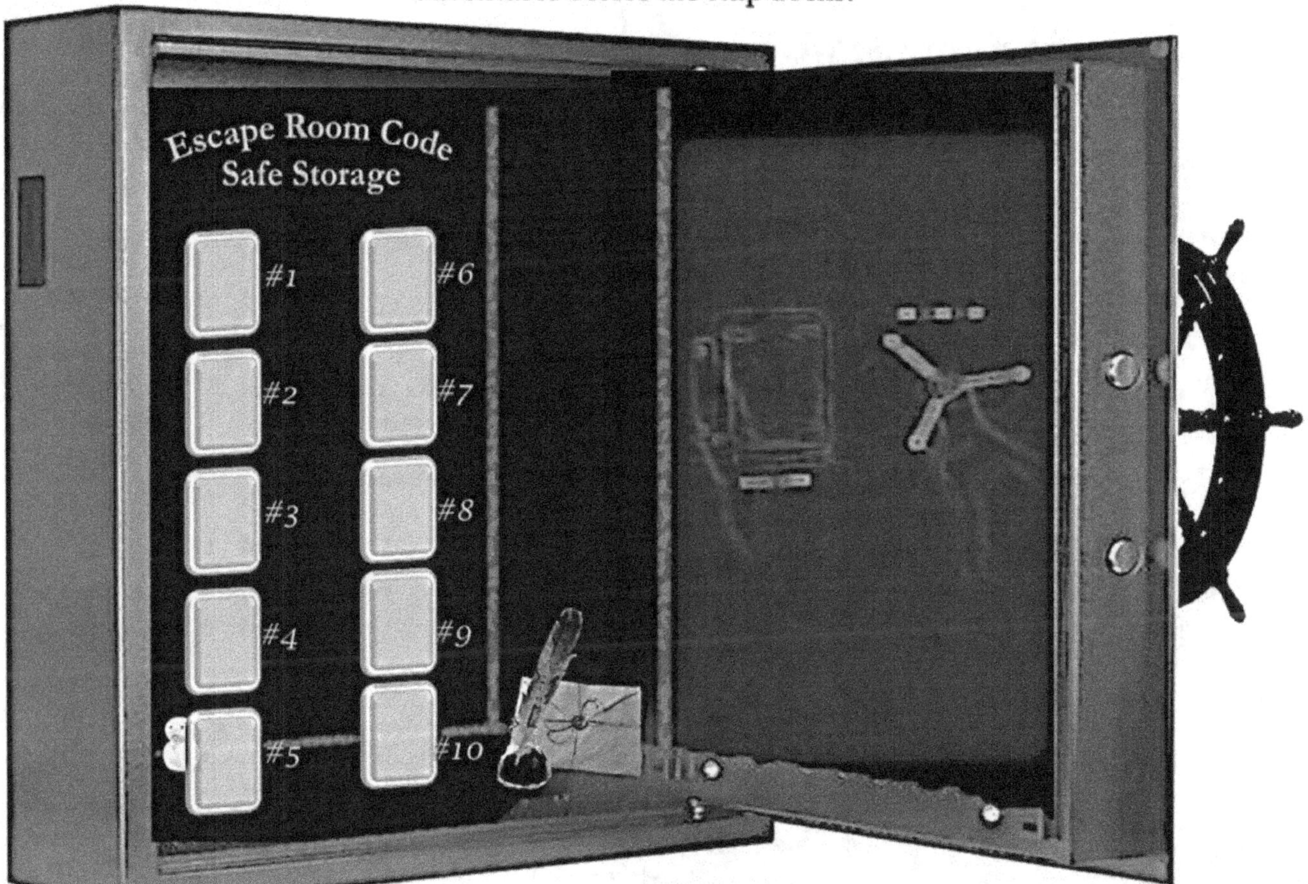

Answers on page 153

ARGH! ME MATEY!
A HIT AND A KICK FOR BEING TOO QUICK!

You have been caught! A letter is in the safe and one last code needs to be sought!

Congratulations for solving the safe code.

I bet you thought that by solving the code to escape the rooms, you would gain a free passage to become the Master Escape Room Cruiser! I am in Knots and Giggles!

Argh! Me matey, I found out who you really are! Sea-curity, Sea-curity, stop these Undersea Shenanigans!

I have been watching you complete every puzzle, and I could not understand how you did it. I had all hands-on deck. I was attending anchor management. Until I found out it was all Nautical nonsense, after my phone was giving me seaworthy notifications. I found it very seagnificant!

Here is a copy of my phone messages
Write on the certificate
who you really are!

Sea you later master code breaker
Hope you are cruising in awhile with
that seafaring smile

Argh! Me matey, sending you details. They are solving every puzzle and making it look too breezy! Something is fishy, I kid you knot!

Crazy! I will get the team onto it. Give us a few days to investigate who they are. They can't be normal guests, going deep diving now!

Don't want to sound too salty, but they are causing waves. Too good to be true, they are sailing sensations!

We have it. They are marine marvels! Be careful with the information, don't be nautical, be nice! We are sending it in code, top sea level clearance! Lock it up in the safe and don't let it go adrift!

Argh! To be sure, to be sure, to be sure! I will lock it up once I crack the code you send. Thanks, me matey!

Xyhi wo$ ....

Di*&qhx W?hpx%

• • • Code converted,
review page 16.
Deletion will occur
in 5 minutes.

To complete your certificate, you will need to write your title (who you really are). Decode the message by going to page 20 for the codes.

Answers on page 153

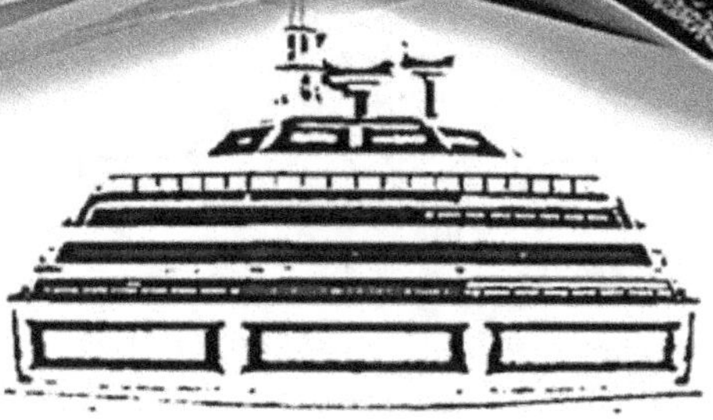

Certificate

of achievement

PROUDLY PRESENTED TO _______ _____:

Write your title here

____

Write your name here

CONGRATULATIONS FOR BECOMING A

MASTER ESCAPE ROOM CRUISER

Answers on page 153

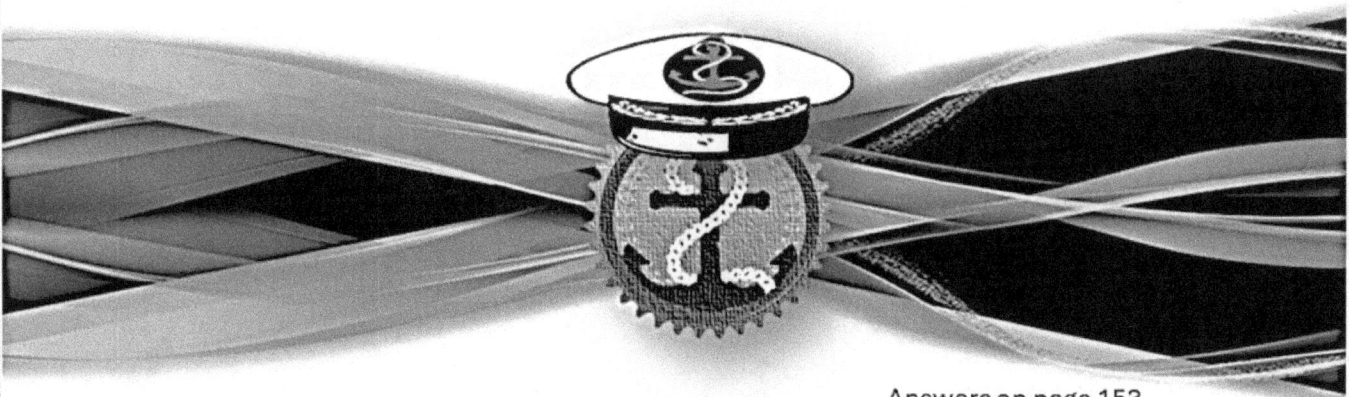

Colouring Time

May you have fair winds and following seas!

For this is how some crew may say goodbye, wishing for a safe journey and an enjoyable breeze.

Palms to the Farm

Colour the picture

CAPTAINS QUARTERS

GLOSSARY OF TERMS

"Most terms are included but are not limited to, this list being provided is not exhaustive and is specific to the cruise ship experience."

Glossary of Terms (words that may be used in this book or on the cruise ship)

Aboard.... You are on the cruise ship, or in other terms you are onboard

About.... When you turn the cruise ship around

Abreast.... To be beside another ship/vessel or a dock

Aft.... Located at the back/rear of the cruise ship

All hands.... All the crew is operational and paying attention on the decks.

Amidship.... The middle of the cruise ship (midship)

Ashore.... Being on land

Astern.... The cruise ship is going in a backward (reverse) direction. The position you or something is on the cruise ship (back). Something is behind the cruise ship

Back-to-back.... Some cruisers stay on the cruise ship after the set voyage. (also known as B2B) Further cruises in a row is known as (B2B2B*****)

Ballast.... Added weight placed to lower the cruise ships centre of gravity, which increases stability and control of the cruise ship.

Beam.... The maximum measure of the width of the cruise ship (measures the size and weight). Typically measured from the waterline.

Berth.... Where the cruise ship is docked in port. Or a bed where you sleep on the cruise ship.

Bow.... The front part of the cruise ship. The direction is forward when you are facing the bow.

Bollard.... Posts on docks/piers/quays/wharfs, used for the mooring lines to keep the cruise ship secure.

Bridge.... The location where the captain and crew steers, controls, and navigates the cruise ship

Bulkhead.... An upright wall within the hull of the cruise ship that divides the ship's interior

Buoy....A marker or float used on the water to identify landmarks for the cruise ship to navigate safely. Also, a lifebuoy is a life-saving device designed to be thrown to a person in the water to keep them afloat and prevent drowning.

Cabin.... The room where you sleep on the cruise ship (Berthing/stateroom). There may be a Luxury Suite, balcony, inside(internal), porthole/window/Oceanview room.

Cabin steward.... The person responsible for the housekeeping by cleaning the cabins/stateroom and attending to guests' requests.

Captain.... Person in charge of the cruise ship, responsible for the crew and passengers' safety.

Cast off.... To release the lines attached to a pier so the cruise ship is released from its mooring.

Chandler....A ship service provider, also known as a ship chandler, offers a wide range of supplies and equipment for cruise ships when docked. This includes maintenance, food, and other necessary cargos or services for ships while at port.

Channel.... The deepest part of the waterway, harbour (harbor)

Companionway.... The stairway inside the cruise ship that connects the deck levels.

Concessionaire.... The businesses that are contracted to conduct services on board the cruise ship. For example, you may recognise them to oversee some shops, photography, art auctions, spa and beauty service

Course.... The cruise ship's route from one port or destination to the next.

Glossary of Terms (continued)

Cruise card.... Provides access to your room; identification (ID) card, and it is a method of payment.

Cruise Director.... Crew member who oversees/organises the ship's activities and entertainment. Also, the Emcee, for most major entertainment events on the cruise ship.

Davit....A small, onboard crane that lowers lifeboats into the water.

Debark.... To leave (depart) the cruise ship.

Deck.... Each level (floor) of the cruise ship.

Disembark.... To leave the cruise ship and go ashore.

Dock.... Structure next to a pier where the cruise ship is loaded, unloaded with; people, goods, & services.

Draft or Draught.... The vertical distance (measured) from the waterline to the (Keel) lowest part of the cruise ship. The depth of water the ship needs so it does not touch the ocean floor.

Dry Dock.... Where the cruise ship is under construction, maintenance, or repair. The ship may enter a section that is emptied and refilled of water.

Embark.... To board the ship.

Fantail.... The overhang at the stern of the ship.

Fathom....A nautical unit of measurement equal to six feet

Fleet....A group of cruise ships travelling together, or under the same ownership.

Forward.... At the front of a cruise ship, facing the bow.

Friends of Bill....A support network of recovering alcoholics, founded by William (Bll) Wilson. (alcoholics anonymous).

Friends of Dorothy....A support and social gathering for the LGBTQIA+ community.

Funnel.... Also known as exhaust funnels or stacks, seen on the upper decks. Exhaust pipes are for all the different machinery found inside the cruise ship. Some funnels are not used and are only for decoration.

Galley.... The cruise ship's kitchen.

Gangway.... The walkway between the cruise ship and the shore, to embark or disembark from the ship.

Gratuities.... A service fee. This may be a part of the fare price or an additional charge.

Gross registered ton (grt).... A measurement of the total enclosed area. The volume of space within the hull and enclosed space above the deck.

Hand.... Crewmember.

Head.... Bathroom.

Helm.... Area of the bridge on which the steering is located.

Hold.... Cruise ship's cargo area

Hotel manager.... Director of hotel operations. Usually responsible for the performance of the Galley, Dining room, Bars, Housekeeping, Pursers, Crew/Public areas, onboard purchasing, ordering and storage, revenue and cost control, Medical, Entertainment and all onboard pax (passenger) related matters.

Hull.... The watertight outer body of the vessel.

Jargon/Lingo....A set of words that may not be understood by others but may be within the cruise industry. Lingo refers to an entire language, dialect or accent.

Glossary of Terms (continued)

Keel.... The large steel beam piece of the bottom of the ship that has the hull attached to it (helps keep the cruise ship upright).

Knot....A unit of speed at which the cruise ship travels, which is one nautical mile per hour. Also, known as when you tie a piece of rope (line), to itself or to something else, that forms a secure hold.

Lanyard.... An accessory worn to hang your cruise card around your neck.

Latitude.... The key factor in the cruise ship's position. The distance north or south of the equator expressed in degrees.

League....A unit of measurement equal to 3.45 nautical miles (5.556km's) at sea. Jules Verne's "20,000 Leagues Under the Sea" does not refer to a depth, but to the distance travelled.

Leeward.... The opposite side of the ship which the wind/weather comes. The downwind side. Pronounced Loo'ard.

Lido..... Usually the deck where the open outdoor pools are located.

Life rafts..... Evacuation rafts (usually automatic).

Lines.... The ropes used to tie up the cruise ship while it is at the dock.

Longitude.... The distance east or west. Lines of longitude, also called meridians, are imaginary lines that divide the Earth. They run north to south from pole to pole, but they measure the distance east or west. Longitude is measured in degrees, minutes, and seconds.

Main Dining Room.... Also known as the MDR, which is the main dining room of the cruise ship.

Maiden voyage.... The first voyage of a new cruise ship.

Maiden call.... The first port on the cruise ship's maiden voyage.

Maître d'.... Crew member responsible for the dining room.

Master.... The Captain, person who oversees the cruise ship.

Midship.... Middle of the cruise ship.

Moor.... To hold (secure) the cruise ship in place with lines.

Mooring....A place where the cruise ship is tied, for example to the dock or wharf.

Nautical Mile.... Based on the Earth's longitude and latitude coordinates, with one nautical mile equalling one minute of latitude.

Muster.... To assemble the passengers and crew.

Muster drill....A mandatory event where passengers assemble in a specific location and receive instructions on what to do in an emergency or acknowledge their understanding of the E-muster...which is an online muster that may include learning safety instructions via an app.

Muster station.... A meeting place onboard the ship where a passenger would assemble, be marked off the muster list, and in the unlikelihood of an emergency, be directed to the allocated lifeboats.

Onboard.... Situated on board the cruise ship.

On Board Credit (OBC).... Having money on your onboard account to spend.

Passageway....A hallway inside the cruise ship.

Passenger space ratio.... The number of 'GRT' divided by the total passenger capacity.

Glossary of Terms (continued)

Passenger to crew ratio.... The total number of passengers divided by the total number of crew.

Pax.... Passengers on the cruise ship.

Personal flotation device (PFD).... Also known as a lifejacket. The device will keep the passenger afloat in the water, increasing their likelihood of survival.

Pitch.... The movement of the cruise ship of going up and down. The rising and falling of the ship's stern and bow (usually during bad weather).

Port.... The left side of the cruise ship when facing forward; also known as the harbour where a ship docks.

Porthole.... A round window on a cruise ship.

Port-of-call.... Where the cruise ship anchors or moors, and the passengers may disembark.

Porter.... Crew member on land to help with luggage before you are embarking on the cruise ship.

Pratique.... Permission given by a port for the cruise ship to enter once it has been certified free of infectious disease by that Country's health authorities.

Promenade.... A deck that extends from bow to stern, on both sides, and may be an open area to the outside, for walking or entering lifeboats. Also, where passenger's stroll along a thoroughfare.

Purser.... Crew member in charge of administration of accounts and money. Duties may include accounting of cash during each sailing.

Quays.... A platform lying alongside or in the water for loading and unloading the cruise ships.

Radomes.... These are the large white balls on top of cruise ships. The name is broken into two parts; the Radar and Dome. The dome covers important equipment such as; the radar, satellite and navigational hardware, protecting them from the weather. Their position is essential for the ship's communications.

Sail away.... The time when the cruise ship sails away from the shore.

Screw.... The cruise ship's propeller. It converts the rotational energy from the ship's engine into the forward thrust.

Sea day.... A full day at sea where the ship does not visit a port.

Stabiliser.... A retractable fin located below the waterline mid-ship, which can be extended to counteract the forces of the ship's motion in the sea.

Starboard.... The right side of the ship, facing forward.

Stateroom.... A cabin.

Stern/aft.... This is the rear part of a ship.

Take the Con.... To take control the navigational duties on the bridge of the ship.

Tender.... A small boat used to transport passengers from the ship to the shore.

Wake.... Waves created by the hull of the ship as it moves through the water. Usually begins at the front as water is displaced by the bow

Windward.... The direction from which the wind is blowing. A windward vessel refers to one that is upwind of another vessel; a leeward vessel is downwind. Windward Pronounced Wind'ard.

Zodiac.... An inflatable raft used by ships to transport passengers ashore. Usually in remote areas such as the Antarctica.

Photo or drawing page

Your Cruise Travel Journal

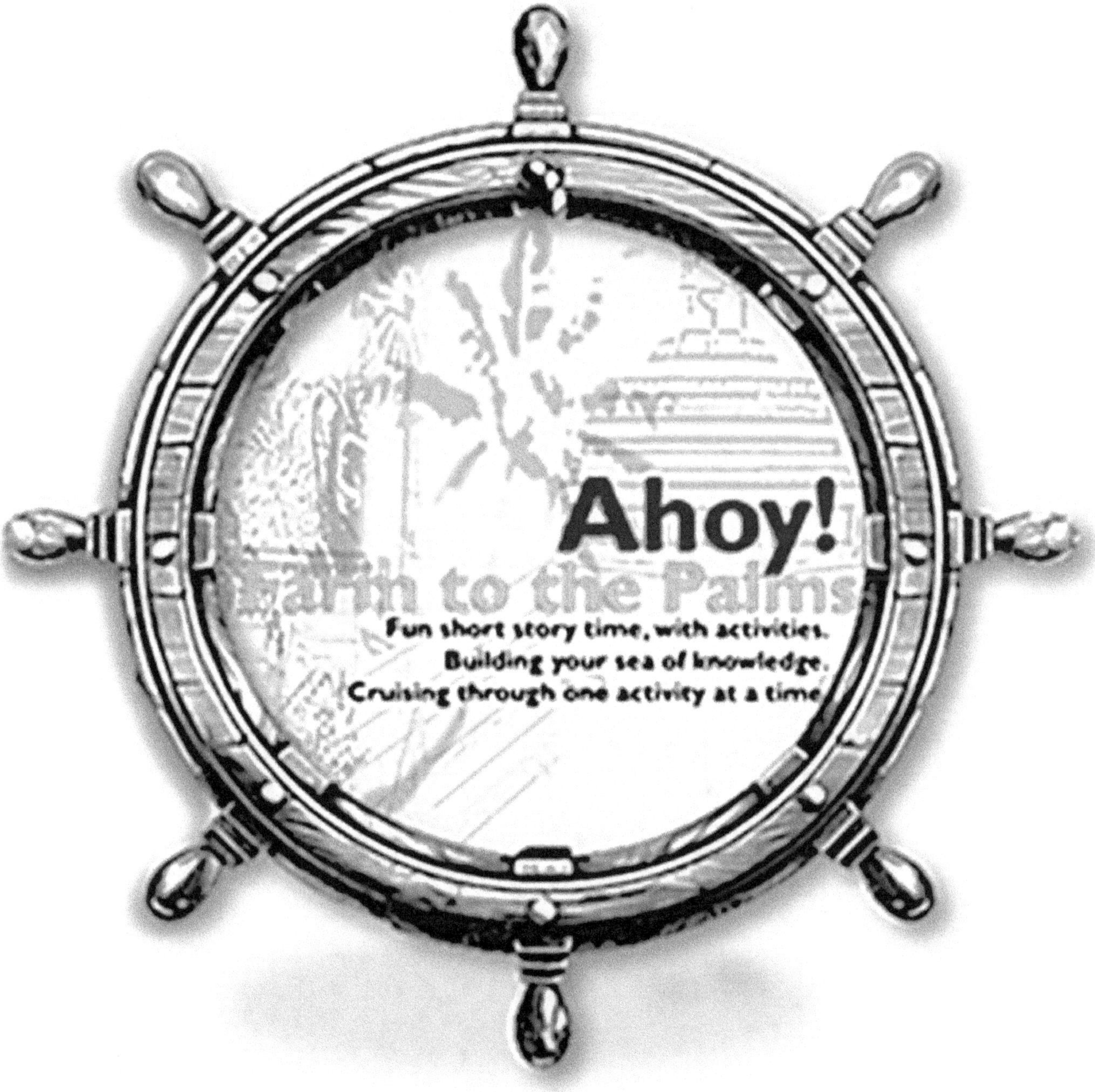

Ahoy!

Fun short story time, with activities.
Building your sea of knowledge.
Cruising through one activity at a time!

Photo or drawing page

Your adventure sails into fun times
Your Cruise Daily Planner

MON	TUE	WED	THU	FRI	SAT	SUN
Kids club					Games room	
			Island Time			
	Disco					

My Cruise Calendar

Cindy forgets what happens each day, so help her write what is planned, for when you would like to rest or play.

DATE	Sunday	Monday	Tuesday	Wednesday	Thursday	Friday	Saturday

My Cruise Calendar
Continued

DATE	Sunday	Monday	Tuesday	Wednesday	Thursday	Friday	Saturday

My Cruise Calendar
Continued

DATE	Sunday	Monday	Tuesday	Wednesday	Thursday	Friday	Saturday

Your Journal Time

Your Itinerary Quick View				
Date	Day	Port	Sea	Port Name
		Port ☐	Sea ☐	
		Port ☐	Sea ☐	
		Port ☐	Sea ☐	
		Port ☐	Sea ☐	
		Port ☐	Sea ☐	
		Port ☐	Sea ☐	
		Port ☐	Sea ☐	
		Port ☐	Sea ☐	
		Port ☐	Sea ☐	
		Port ☐	Sea ☐	
		Port ☐	Sea ☐	
		Port ☐	Sea ☐	
		Port ☐	Sea ☐	
		Port ☐	Sea ☐	
		Port ☐	Sea ☐	
		Port ☐	Sea ☐	
		Port ☐	Sea ☐	
		Port ☐	Sea ☐	
		Port ☐	Sea ☐	
		Port ☐	Sea ☐	
		Port ☐	Sea ☐	
		Port ☐	Sea ☐	
		Port ☐	Sea ☐	

Pictures

My journal notes

Draw or paste a picture

Port Day

Boarding Day — Circle the weather for the day

Day [   ] — Circle the weather for the day

Tick a box [ ] Port Day [ ] Sea Day

WRITE YOUR OWN STORY AND DRAW PICTURES

My journal notes

Pictures

Draw or paste a picture

Tick a box ☐ Port Day ☐ Sea Day

Day [ ]   Circle the weather for the day

Day [ ]   Circle the weather for the day

Tick a box ☐ Port Day ☐ Sea Day

WRITE YOUR OWN STORY AND DRAW PICTURES

Pictures

My journal notes

Draw or paste a picture

Day ☐ Circle the weather for the day

Tick a box ☐ Port Day ☐ Sea Day

Day ☐ Circle the weather for the day

Tick a box ☐ Port Day ☐ Sea Day

WRITE YOUR OWN STORY AND DRAW PICTURES

My journal notes

Pictures

Draw or paste a picture

Tick a box ☐ Port Day ☐ Sea Day

Tick a box ☐ Port Day ☐ Sea Day

Day [ ]   Circle the weather for the day

Day [ ]   Circle the weather for the day

WRITE YOUR OWN STORY AND DRAW PICTURES

Pictures

My journal notes

Draw or paste a picture

Tick a box ☐ Port Day ☐ Sea Day

Day [____]   Circle the weather for the day

Tick a box ☐ Port Day ☐ Sea Day

Day [____]   Circle the weather for the day

WRITE YOUR OWN STORY AND DRAW PICTURES

My journal notes

Pictures

Draw or paste a picture

Tick a box ☐ Port Day ☐ Sea Day

Day [   ] Circle the weather for the day

Tick a box ☐ Port Day ☐ Sea Day

Day [   ] Circle the weather for the day

WRITE YOUR OWN STORY AND DRAW PICTURES

Pictures

My journal notes

Draw or paste a picture

Day [   ] Circle the weather for the day

Tick a box [ ] Port Day [ ] Sea Day

Tick a box [ ] Port Day [ ] Sea Day

Day [   ] Circle the weather for the day

WRITE YOUR OWN STORY AND DRAW PICTURES

My journal notes

Pictures

Draw or paste a picture

Day ▢ Circle the weather for the day

Tick a box ▢ Port Day ▢ Sea Day

Day ▢ Circle the weather for the day

Tick a box ▢ Port Day ▢ Sea Day

WRITE YOUR OWN STORY AND DRAW PICTURES

Pictures

My journal notes

Draw or paste a picture

Day _____   Circle the weather for the day

Tick a box ☐ Port Day   ☐ Sea Day

Day _____   Circle the weather for the day

Tick a box ☐ Port Day   ☐ Sea Day

WRITE YOUR OWN STORY AND DRAW PICTURES

My journal notes

Pictures

Draw or paste a picture

Tick a box ☐ Port Day ☐ Sea Day

Day [____] Circle the weather for the day

Tick a box ☐ Port Day ☐ Sea Day

Day [____] Circle the weather for the day

WRITE YOUR OWN STORY AND DRAW PICTURES

Pictures

My journal notes

Draw or paste a picture

Day ☐ Circle the weather for the day

Tick a box ☐ Port Day ☐ Sea Day

Day ☐ Circle the weather for the day

Tick a box ☐ Port Day ☐ Sea Day

WRITE YOUR OWN STORY AND DRAW PICTURES

Pictures

My journal notes

Draw or paste a picture

Day ☐ Circle the weather for the day

Tick a box ☐ Port Day ☐ Sea Day

Day ☐ Circle the weather for the day

Tick a box ☐ Port Day ☐ Sea Day

WRITE YOUR OWN STORY AND DRAW PICTURES

Photo or drawing page

Colour the picture

Your Port/Island Time

Colour the picture

My Port/Island Time

Pictures

Island/Place/Country Culture

Draw or paste a picture

Differences to your culture (food, clothes, living etc.)

WRITE YOUR OWN STORY AND DRAW PICTURES

My Port/Island Time

Pictures

Draw or paste a picture

Island/Place/Country Culture

Differences to your culture (food, clothes, living etc.)

WRITE YOUR OWN STORY AND DRAW PICTURES

My Port/Island Time

Pictures

Draw or paste a picture

Island/Place/Country Culture

Differences to your culture (food, clothes, living etc.)

WRITE YOUR OWN STORY AND DRAW PICTURES

Journal Time

Your new friends

My new friends

Name:	Name:
Address:	Address:
Phone:	Phone:
Social Media and other contacts:	Social Media and other contacts:

Name:	Name:
Address:	Address:
Phone:	Phone:
Social Media and other contacts:	Social Media and other contacts:

BECOME A PEN PAL, BUT MAKE SURE YOUR PARENTS KNOW WHAT YOU ARE WRITING HERE NOW.

My new friends

Name:
Address:
Phone:
Social Media and other contacts:

Name:
Address:
Phone:
Social Media and other contacts:

Name:
Address:
Phone:
Social Media and other contacts:

Name:
Address:
Phone:
Social Media and other contacts:

BECOME A PEN PAL, BUT MAKE SURE YOUR PARENTS KNOW WHAT YOU ARE WRITING HERE NOW.

Photo or drawing page

Shhhhh!

This is the answer sheet. Isn't this a nice treat!

Answers Time

Page 9

Page 12
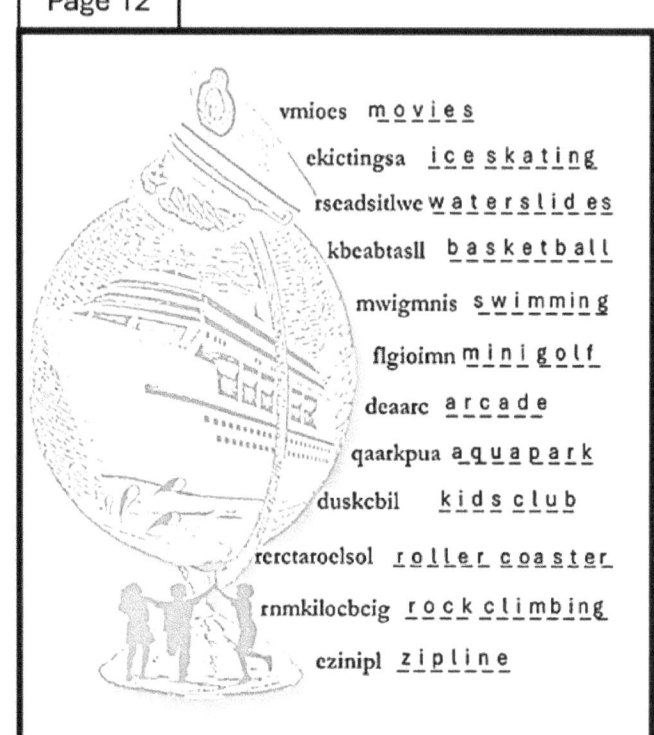

- vmiocs — m o v i e s
- ekictingsa — i c e s k a t i n g
- rscadsitlwe — w a t e r s l i d e s
- kbeabtasll — b a s k e t b a l l
- mwigmnis — s w i m m i n g
- flgioimn — m i n i g o l f
- deaarc — a r c a d e
- qaarkpua — a q u a p a r k
- duskcbil — k i d s c l u b
- rerctaroclsol — r o l l e r c o a s t e r
- rnmkilocbcig — r o c k c l i m b i n g
- ezinipl — z i p l i n e

Page 17
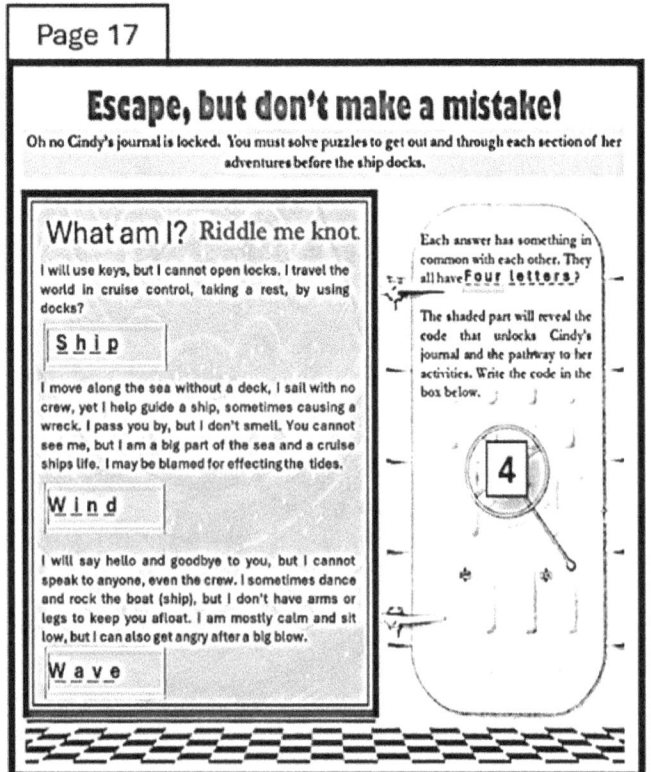

Page 18
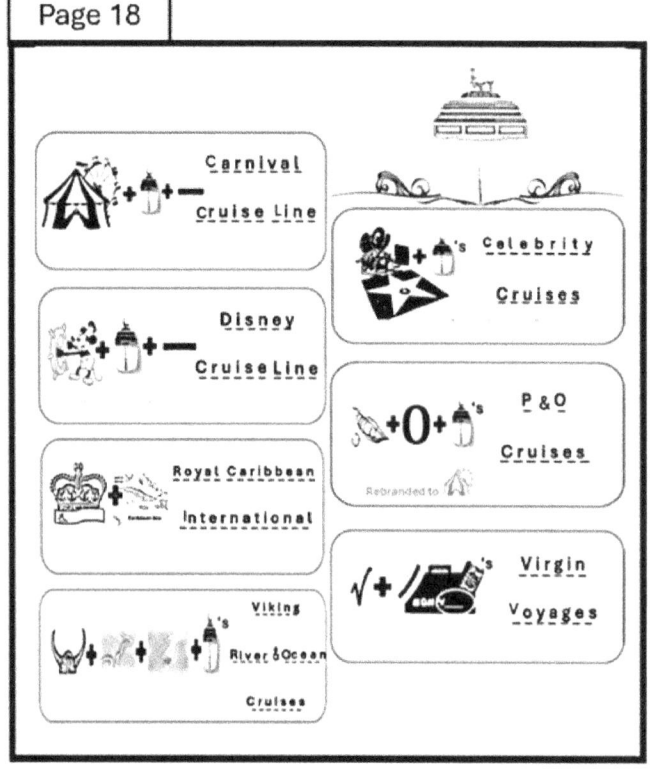

Answers Time

Page 20

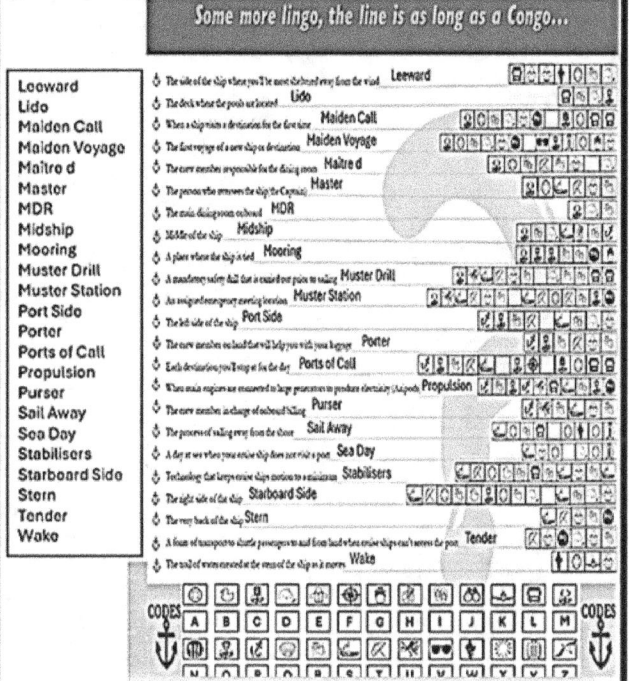

Page 21

Page 25

Page 27

Answers Time

Page 28

These Ship jokes will make you laugh for Shore!
The shuttle driver loves to tell lots of dad jokes during your tour.

What did the students get on the cruise ship?
Answer: **A scholarship**

What did the beach say when the tide came in?
Answer: **Long time no sea**

The cruise ship is fully booked but there isn't a single person on board. How?
Answer: **All are married**

How do you disembark before even embarking onto a cruise ship? You have not boarded yet?
Answer: **You read a dictionary**

What is the name of the optometrist on a cruise ship?
Answer: **'Sea'farer**

Where do you take a sick cruise ship?
Answer: **To the dock**

Why did the cruise ship leave the port early?
Answer: **Pier Pressure**

What medication did the doctor give to the Captain?
Answer: **Vitamin Sea**

What game is played every 100 years on a cruise ship?
Answer: **Sail of the century**

What do a fleet of cruise ships have in common?
Answer: **A relationship**

What did the ocean say to the cruise ship?
Answer: **Nothing, it just waved**

Why did the Captain cancel the trip to the Bluetooth iceberg?
Answer: **It was not in sync**

Where does a cruise ship get fuel at sea?
Answer: **Shell service (gas) station**

What do the sailors use to clean their noses when they have a cold?
Answer: **Anchorchief**

Why was the Captain too full to eat during a storm?
Answer: **Was too 'blow'ted**

How can you tell when the ocean is friendly?
Answer: **It waves**

What type of cruise ship is the best to cruise with?
Answer: **A Friendship**

What is another name for a fit cruise ship?
Answer: **Ship shape**

What did the Captain say when he was asked why he wasn't leaving the port?
Answer: **I haven't got a crew**

What vessel won the tug-a-war game?
Answer: **Tugboat**

Page 29

Circle the right answer.

What would you be travelling on if you wanted to go on a holiday that has a kids club?

| Yacht | **Ocean Liner** | Cargo Ship |
| Warship | Submarine | Houseboat |

On what cruise line will you see Donald Duck?

| Virgin | Carnival | Princess |
| **Disney** | P&O | Royal Caribbean |

What Cruise has (had) the Wiggles?

| Virgin | Carnival | Princess |
| Oceania | P&O | **Royal Caribbean** |

A child is allowed to press buttons in the elevator, but not here?

| Pool | Dining Room | Buffet |
| Kids Club | **Casino** | Music Hall |

Who was the first ever "Godfather" of a cruise ship?

| 50 Cent | Justin Bieber | **PitBull** |
| Bruno Mars | Ed Sheeran | Luke Combs |

What Cruise line has (had) Dr. Seuss?

| Virgin | **Carnival** | Princess |
| Oceania | P&O | Royal Caribbean |

What is the busiest cruise port?

| Sydney | New York | **Miami** |
| Santorini | Dover | Nassau |

What cruise ship is taboo (not talked about)?

| Mothership | Friendship | Warship |
| Carriership | **Titanic** | Cargo Ship |

What is the brig on a ship?

| **Jail/Gaol** | Kitchen | Cabin |
| Toilet | Bridge | Bar |

Which feature on a ship may be fake/not used?

| Engine | Anchor | Lines/ropes |
| Captain | Food | **Funnel** |

Some cruise ships are missing this deck number?

| One | Three | Five |
| Eight | **Thirteen** | Eleven |

What are some toilets called on ships?

| Brigs | Galley | Dish |
| **Heads** | Bridge | Flush |

Page 30

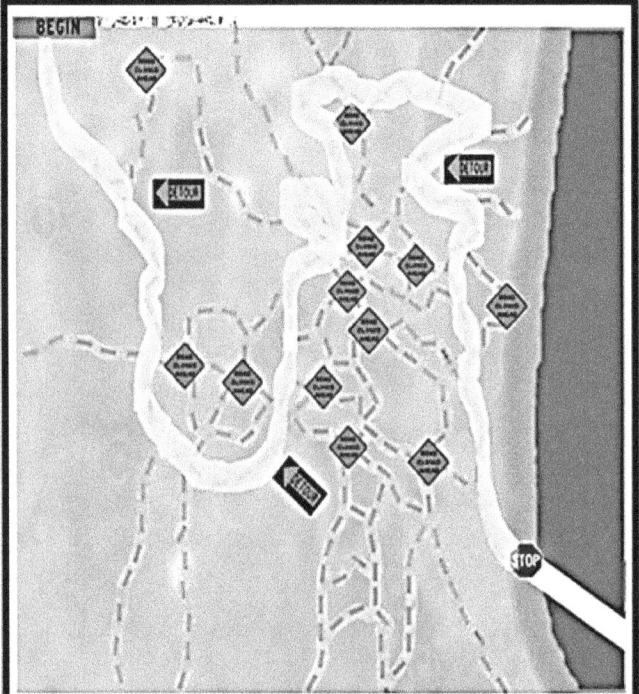

Page 31

Welcome to the Port, the area Where
YOU ARE ABOUT TO BOARD

```
        T       A
        H       R        Y
        R               O
W H E R E     A B O U T
E               A        O
L               B       O
C               O    A R E
P O R T         A
M               R
T H E           D
```

W	E	L	C	O	M	E		T	O		T	H	E
A1	D5	K8	N1	E14	I6	J4		B15	H4		E8	E1	F6

P	O	R	T		T	H	E		A	R	E	A
I1	L14	O2	M7		O10	M5	H9		G14	F12	B1	I8

W	H	E	R	E		Y	O	U		A	R	E
B11	M10	J10	J2	O2		B4	N8	K15		O4	I12	F3

A	B	O	U	T		T	O		B	O	A	R	D
K1	A11	L3	N13	A3		I15	C8		O15	B4	J13	C3	H2

144

Page 32

FIND A WORD

Find these words whilst travelling to the ship, it will keep you safe during your holiday trip.
After you have completed your road safety test, there will be 13 spaces left.
It is our message to you, before you venture into something new.

C	A	R	A	D	I	A	T	O	R	O	A	D	S
O	R	L	T	H	R	E	E	G	R	E	E	N	C
R	I	I	O	S	A	F	E	I	A	M	B	E	R
N	G	S	P	R	E	D	Y	V	S	T	O	P	O
E	H	T	B	I	K	E	S	E	R	U	L	E	S
R	T	E	E	N	J	O	Y	W	L	E	F	T	S
S	Z	N	T	I	M	E	O	A	S	L	O	W	I
H	F	W	A	T	C	H	U	Y	K	N	O	W	N
I	O	T	O	U	R	C	R	U	I	S	E	W	G
P	L	O	O	K	C	A	R	S	R	A	D	I	O
M	L	S	P	E	E	D	F	D	R	I	V	E	L
A	O	L	I	M	I	T	S	F	V	E	E	R	O
T	W	H	E	E	L	V	E	H	I	C	L	E	S
E	S	E	A	T	B	E	L	T	S	C	A	R	T

Page 33

FIND A WORD

- **SLOW** down when passing emergency vehicles and pull out of the way when they need to pass.
- A safe driver always **FOLLOWS** the road rules.
- Keep a safe distance from **BIKES**
- You must always adhere to the road **RULES**
- Maps are good to use as they prevent you from getting **LOST**
- A vehicle sliding on ice may **VEER** out of control. It is important to drive to the road conditions, as it prevents injury and a permanent **SCAR**
- You cross the road using a **ZEBRA**/pedestrian **CROSSING**
- If you go on a **TOUR** at a cruise port, make sure you are with a safe and licenced driver.
- When crossing the road, you should **LOOK LISTEN** and **WATCH**
- Some countries drive on the **LEFT** while others on the **RIGHT** side of the road, which also means the steering **WHEEL** is on opposite sides.
- Always allow enough **TIME** for your trip and don't rush.
- **GIVE WAY** may mean that you slow down or stop to let another vehicle or pedestrian pass.
- There are three Traffic signals:
  1. **RED** light means stop
  2. **AMBER** or also known as **YELLOW** light means slow down and prepare to stop.
  3. **GREEN** light means go.
- Watch out for the **VEHICLES** ahead, just in case they slow down or stop.
- Animals are **KNOWN** to cross the roads, keeping an eye on your surroundings will help everyone in the **CAR**.
- **GIVE** yourself a break, stop and refresh during long distance trips.
- A **STOP** sign means all cars must stop completely and then proceed when it is **SAFE**
- For safety of all road users, you must obey the **SPEED LIMITS**
- Never have the **CARS RADIO** turned up loud as you may not hear emergency vehicles or keep on **TOP** of your surroundings.
- It is suggested to leave a **THREE** second distance between cars.
- All passengers must wear a **SEAT BELT** as it keeps you safe.
- It is always good, if you are a child, to watch adults **DRIVE** as this will help you when you go for your licence.
- It is safer to slow down when you go around **CORNERS**
- You must obey **TRAFFIC** controllers

Page 37

Escape, but don't make a mistake!

Oh no Cindy's journal is locked. You must solve puzzles to get out and through each section of her adventures before the ship docks.

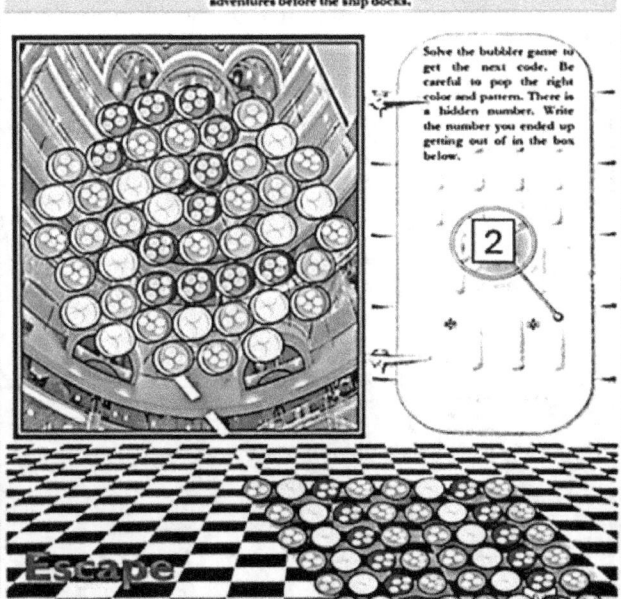

Solve the bubbler game to get the next code. Be careful to pop the right color and pattern. There is a hidden number. Write the number you ended up getting out of in the box below.

2

Page 41

[Color-by-number grid puzzle solution]

Answers Time

Page 42

Ahoy!
A fun way to keep you safe, and a float like a buoy.

A muster drill is to show you what to do if there was a real **emergency**. The muster station crew leaders will tell you about how to put on a **life jacket**, where the **muster stations** are, and they will explain other emergency information on the ship. This may be done in **person** or on an **app**.

Word search answers (highlighted):
- MUSTER
- STATION
- TIME
- PERSON
- EMERGENCY
- JACKET
- LIFE

Page 43

Fill in the blanks using the words on the Bow.

Life jackets are located at the **muster stations**.

Additional jackets are at **lifeboat stations** and on board the **lifeboats** themselves.

Life jackets come in **adult**, **child** and **infant** sizes.

Always check the **weight** and size on the jacket label.

Also, make sure you watch the **muster drill** to know how to wear one.

It is time to keep you safe now.

Word bank:
- Life jackets
- muster stations
- lifeboat stations
- lifeboats
- adult
- child
- infant
- weight
- muster drill

Page 47

Crack the safe in your cabin

1 2 3	None of these numbers are correct or used in any of the code squares.
4 5 6 A	Only one number is correct, and it is in the right place for the letter 'A' square.
7 8 9	Only one number is correct, but it is not in the right place. It is used in the 'B' square.
3 0 2	Only one number is correct, but it is not in the right place. It is used in the 'C' square.
1 7 6 B	Only one number is correct, and it is in the right place for the 'B' square.
8 5 0 C	Only one number is correct and in the right place for the 'C' square.

Crack the safe to get the next code. Write the number that is in the 'B' box into the box below.

In this activity you will need to decode the correct 3-digit code from the hints on the left and then write them in the correct 'ABC' squares.

7

Also, write the code on page 101.

A	B	C
4	7	0

Page 49

Play a little game of Putt Putt and see which player wins the cup.

Some cruise ships may have a mini golf course waiting for you to enjoy a little hit.

The number of strokes you shot represented the largest seabird. Find the Par you shot and the ball you used.

Par **6**   Ball to sink **E**

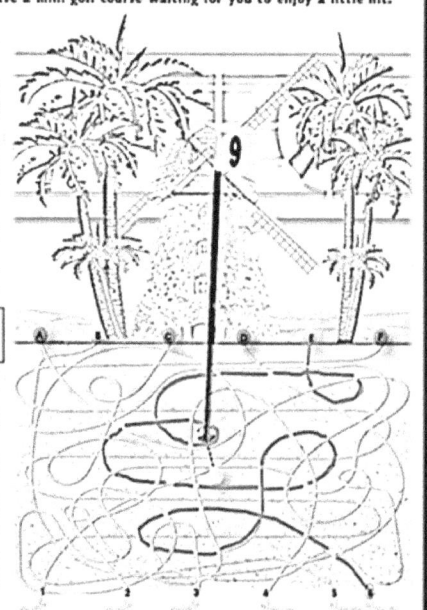

Par – the number of strokes (shots) you are expected to make to get the ball into the hole. Par 9 means you should get the ball into the hole within 9 shots.

Ace (Hole-in-One) – When you hit from the tee into the hole in a single shot.

Condor – four shots below par. On a par 9, you would get the ball into the hole in 5 shots.

Albatross (Double Eagle) – When you hit three shots below par. On a par 9, you would get the ball into the hole in 6 shots.

Eagle – When you hit two shots below par. On a par 9, you would get the ball into the hole in 7 shots.

Birdie – When you shoot one below par. On a par 9, you would get the ball into the hole in 8 shots.

Bogey – When you shoot one over par. On a par 9, you would get the ball into the hole in 10 shots.

Double Bogey – When you shoot two over par. On a par 9, you would get the ball into the hole in 11 shots.

Triple Bogey – When you shoot three over par. On a par 9, you would get the ball into the hole in 12 shots.

Answers Time

Page 53
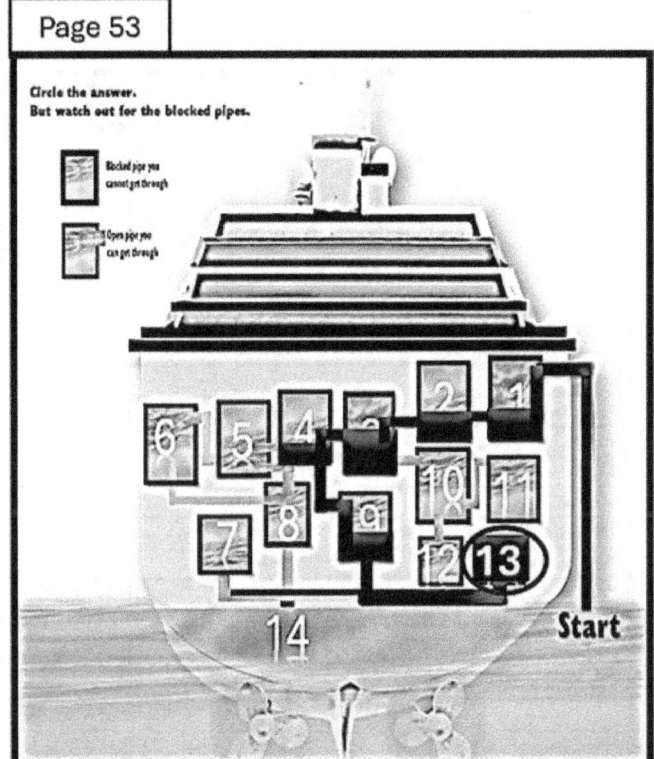

Page 54
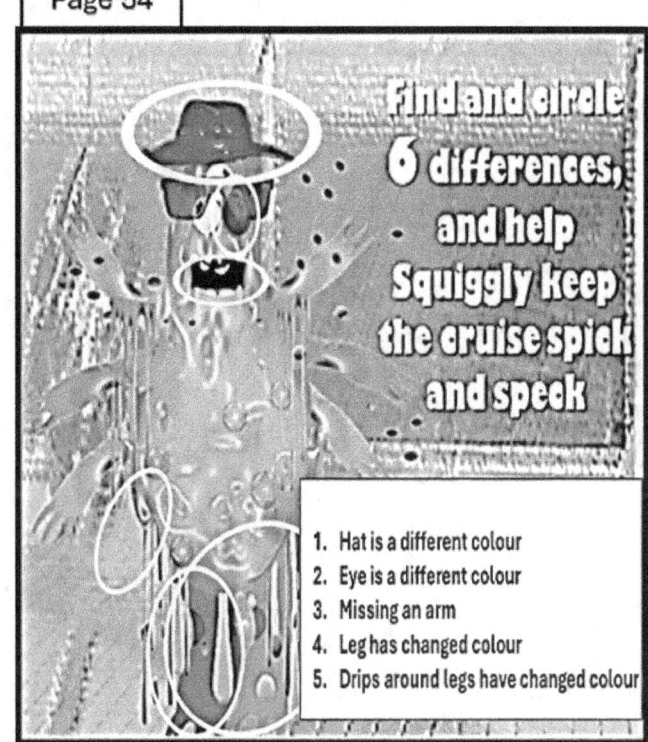

1. Hat is a different colour
2. Eye is a different colour
3. Missing an arm
4. Leg has changed colour
5. Drips around legs have changed colour

Page 57

Page 59
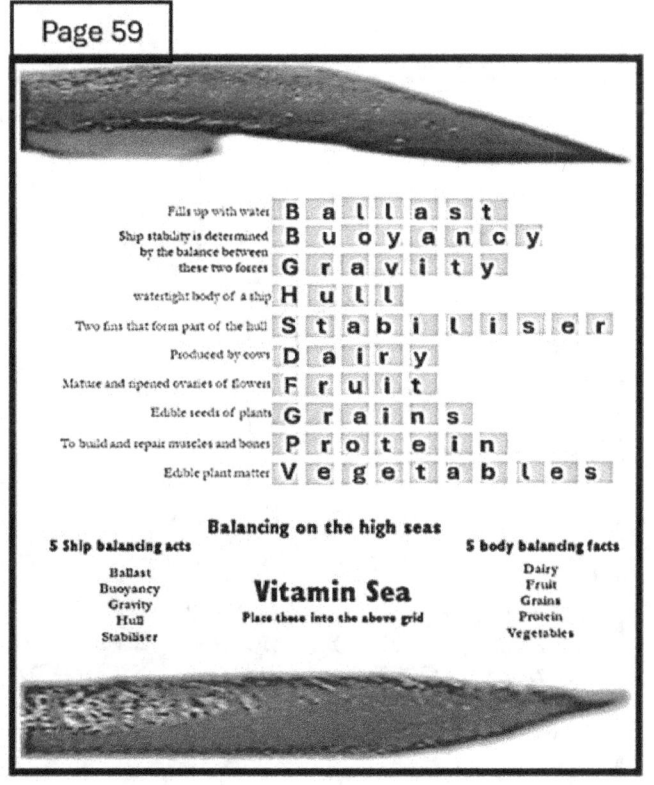

Answers Time

Page 61

Where am I?
DRAW A LINE TO THE CORRECT PLACE ON THE SHIP

Starboard — Bow — Stern — Midship — Forward — Aft — Port

Match the directions and find your way, as you become excited to head to the kids' club to play. Complete both puzzles - the diagram above and the words below by drawing a line.

- Aft — Between the forward and the aft of the ship.
- Bow — The front curve part of the ship that helps cut through water.
- Forward — Front of a cruise ship, facing the bow.
- Midship — Between the forward and the aft of the ship.
- Port — Left side of the ship when facing forward.
- Starboard — Right side of the ship when facing forward.
- Stern — The rear of the ship. Difference between stern and aft is that the aft is onboard whereas the stern is the outside back. / Back of the ship, which is opposite to the Bow.

Page 63

COUNTRY Destination (written in red in the square)	Direction (can only go up and across)	Nautical Miles
Start to Hawaii	North only	6
Hawaii to Greece	East only	4
Greece to Japan	East only	3
Japan to Australia	South only	3
Australia to Fiji	East only	2
Fiji to New Zealand	South and West	3
New Zealand to Vanuatu	North only	3
Vanuatu to Singapore	West only	2
Singapore to the United Kingdom	West and North	6
United Kingdom to Alaska	West only	4
Alaska to United States of America	South and East	2
United States of America to Bahamas	South only	2
	Total Nautical Miles Travelled	40

Page 64

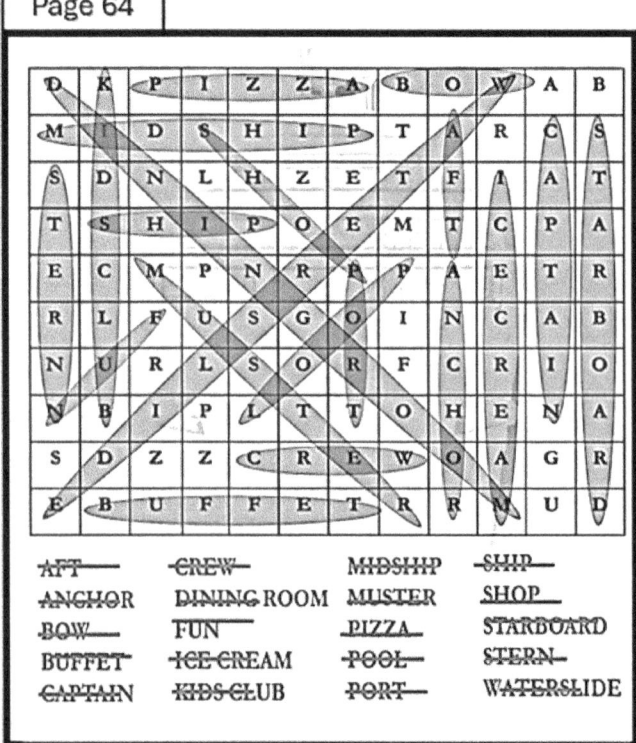

- ~~AFT~~
- ~~ANCHOR~~
- ~~BOW~~
- ~~BUFFET~~
- ~~CAPTAIN~~
- ~~CREW~~
- ~~DINING~~ ROOM
- ~~FUN~~
- ~~ICE CREAM~~
- ~~KIDS CLUB~~
- ~~MIDSHIP~~
- MUSTER
- ~~PIZZA~~
- ~~POOL~~
- ~~PORT~~
- ~~SHIP~~
- SHOP
- ~~STARBOARD~~
- ~~STERN~~
- WATERSLIDE

Page 67

Escape, but don't make a mistake!
Oh no Cindy's journal is locked. You must solve puzzles to get out and through each section of her adventures before the ship docks.

You enter on deck 6; you need to be on 4, but what deck did you get on, when it finally opened the door.

- Deck 9
- Deck 7
- Deck 4
- **Deck 6**

Solve the lift movements to get the next code. Be careful as the lift has a mind of its own. If too many buttons are pressed, it will take you to the unknown. Write the deck you ended up getting out of in the box below.

6

148

Page 68

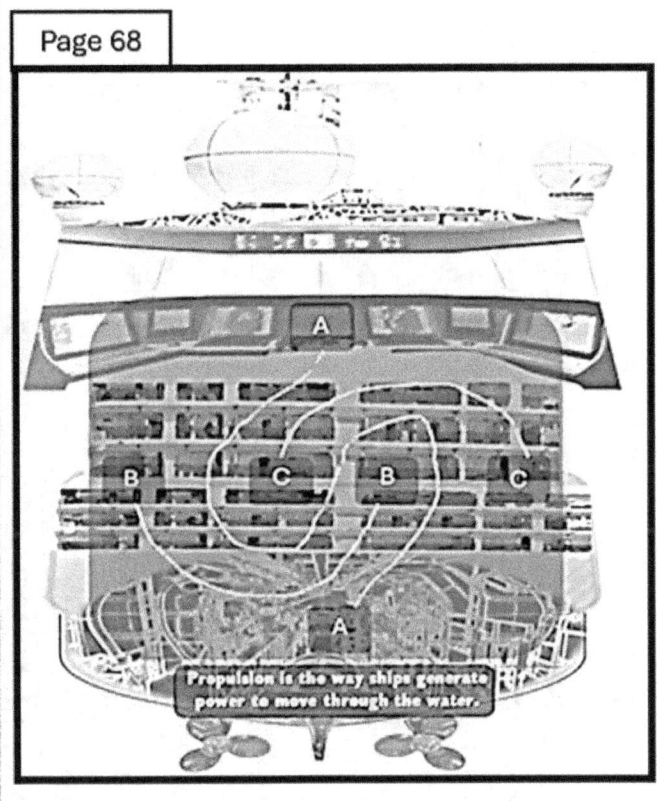

Page 71

Page 74

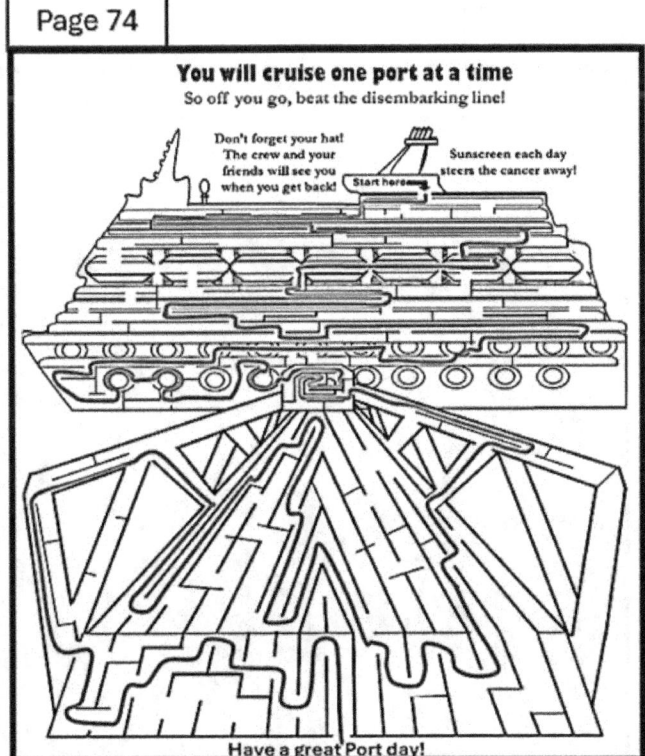

Page 76

There are dolphins following the ship at sea
It's a sign of good luck, find them in this picture and write how many there are here. 16

Answers Time

Page 79

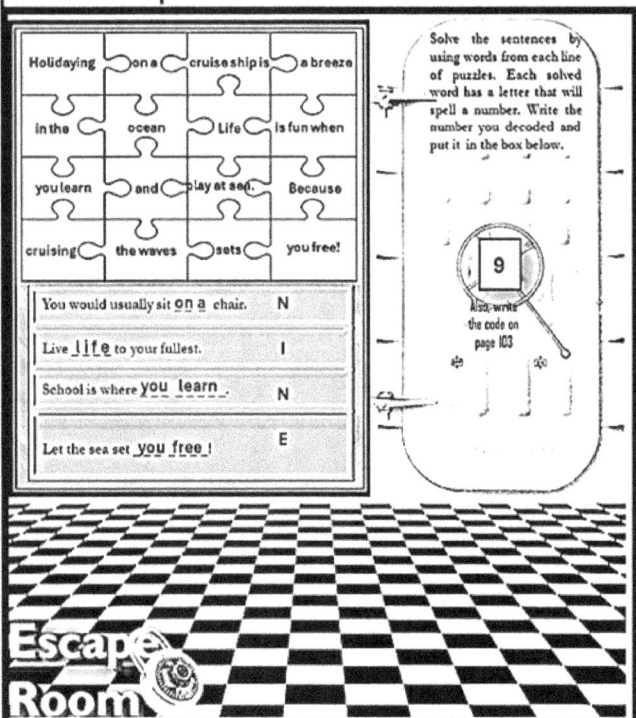

Holidaying	on a cruise ship is a breeze
in the	ocean Life is fun when
you learn	and play at sea. Because
cruising	the waves sets you free!

You would usually sit **on a** chair. — **N**
Live **life** to your fullest. — **I**
School is where **you learn**. — **N**
Let the sea set **you free**! — **E**

Code: **9**

Page 80

Page 81

A MUTINY
ARRR, ON THE PLANK! WHO HAS TAKEN OVER THE RANK?

1. The Chef is in a place that is on deck 10. **Buffet**
2. Squiggly was caught with an item that is used when you are wet. **Towel Animal**
3. The Cabin Crew, like the one that is in the pool, had an item that starts with the letter 'C'. **Cookie**
4. The Captain is either in the pool or sports area. **Sports area**
5. The one that is in the Cabin, also has the towel animal. **Squiggly**
6. Cindy is on deck 12. **Pool**
7. The one on the bridge had the cookie. **Cabin Crew**
8. Squiggly is asleep on deck 3. **Cabin**
9. The Cabin Crew kept leaving crumbs. **Cookie**
10. The Chef had taken a breathing device. **Snorkel**
11. The cheeky one that walks the plank is on Deck 11. **Cabin Crew**

What item was found at the scene of the crime? **Cookie**

Who caused the mutiny? taking the helm. **Cabin Crew**
Oh! They are the cheeky one!

Page 83

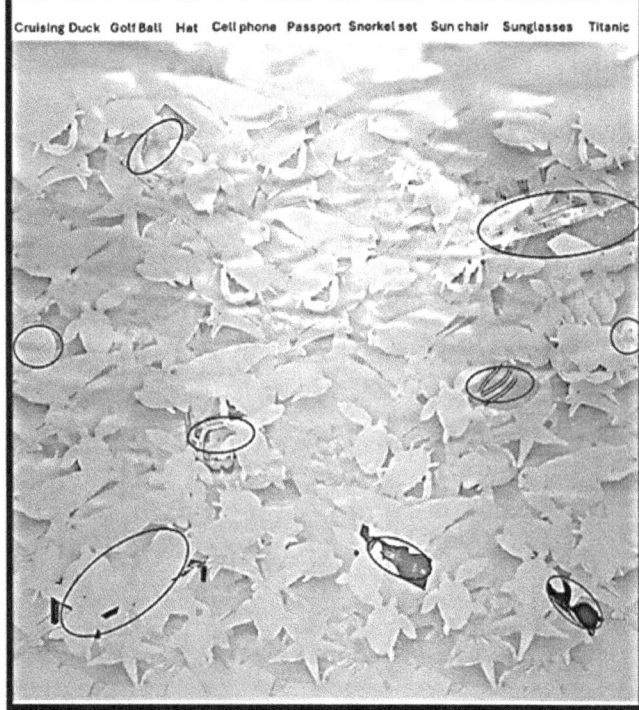

Cruising Duck · Golf Ball · Hat · Cell phone · Passport · Snorkel set · Sun chair · Sunglasses · Titanic

Answers Time

Page 87

Escape, but don't make a mistake!
Oh no Cindy's journal is locked. You must solve puzzles to get out and through each section of her adventures before the ship docks.

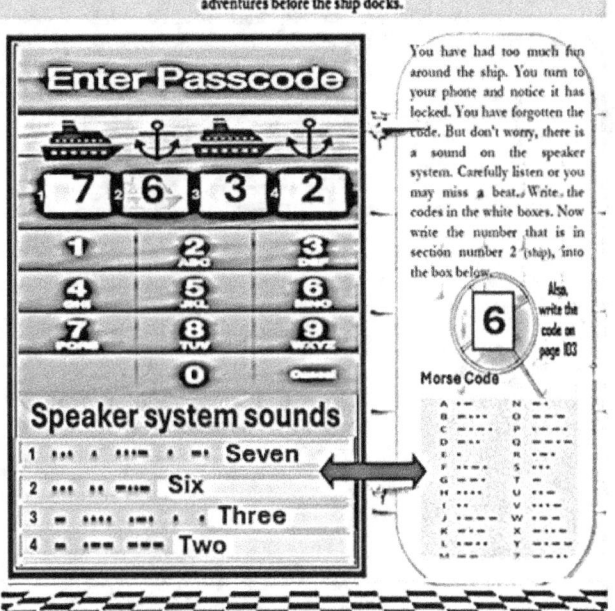

Page 90

Who am I?
Find out who is at the Helm! Make sure the riddles don't make you feel overwhelmed!

Page 91

Who am I?
Riddle me, Riddle not! Can you see the answer on the spot!

I guide you to your destination, pointing you to your vacation. Without me, you may steer astray, relying on me night and day. Who am I? **Compass**

I sail the high seas, but my ship relies on the breeze. I board other vessels without a ticket. I seek treasure but I'm not rich or give you an enjoyable adventure. Who am I? **Pirate**

I have a deck but not a card, I master the sea, where dolphins are my guard. I may dwell, but most think I am swell. Who am I? **Cruise ship**

I stand tall and bright; you will see me mainly at night. You use me so you don't hit the shore, but others like to climb me during their tour. Who am I? **Lighthouse**

I travel the world but have no passport. I have your belongings but never use them. I am always with you when we travel, but I am not your friend. Who am I? **Suitcase**

I am everywhere for you to see, hanging around not wanting to be used, but you need me. An emergency may happen one day where you throw me away, but you must bring me back in. Who am I? **Life ring**

I have both oceans and seas but no water, nor people but I have countries, cities and borders. I am on demand and at your command. Who am I? **Navigation Maps**

I cater for a mob, but I am not in that job. I let people walk all over me, but I am stronger than you see. I keep you safe whilst you embark and disembark. Who am I? **Gangway**

When you need me, you throw me away, but you always take me back. I keep you from going adrift where the sea may pull. Who am I? **Anchor**

I was known to be unsinkable, but in legends of icebergs, my memory lies. A tragic maiden voyage, under cold skies, I am taboo on ships, never to be described. Who am I? **Titanic**

I cover most of the world, where my tops are sometimes curled. I dip deeper than you can go, with sunken ship secrets and myths flow. Who am I? **Ocean**

I keep you on course, navigate, and set cruise control. I used to be a lonely wheel that you manually turned, but now, I am part of bigger things, that automatically returns. Who am I? **Helm**

Cars cross me on land, but here you can only walk and use me to stand. I command and conquer, and cannot go unmanned. Who am I? **Bridge**

One letter from each answer will spell out the final riddle. WHO AM I? **Master Mariner**

Page 92

Quack, Quack, Quack
A farm fun fact! This is what some cruise people may pack!

On Cindy's farm she has ducks named the Campbell's. Her ducks provide them with eggs, and every day they lay, they are cruising in their pond and have no interest in flying away.

On some cruise ships, people hide toy ducks for you to find.

Find out if there are any on your cruise ship, as some may also leave them behind.

Don't be sad if your cruise has no ducks, as some have been hidden in this book, so you can still try your luck.

Beak and Seek
write the pages where the ducks are. There are 60 ducks to find in this whole book. *Hint check from beginning to the end

Record the page number and the **number of ducks** on that page
Include this page. Only count the yellow ducks. Do not count the ducks on any of the answer pages 141-153.

Page #	Ducks	Page #	Ducks	Page #	Ducks	Page #	Ducks	Page #	Ducks
1	1	28	1	52	1	82	1	103	1
8	1	36	1	54	1	83	1	116	1
10	1	38	1	58	1	89	1	119	1
11	1	41	1	69	1	90	1	154	1
13	1	42	1	75	1	92	33	**TOTAL DUCKS**	
23	1	48	1	77	1	102	1	# of Pages 28	Ducks 60

151

Answers Time

Page 95
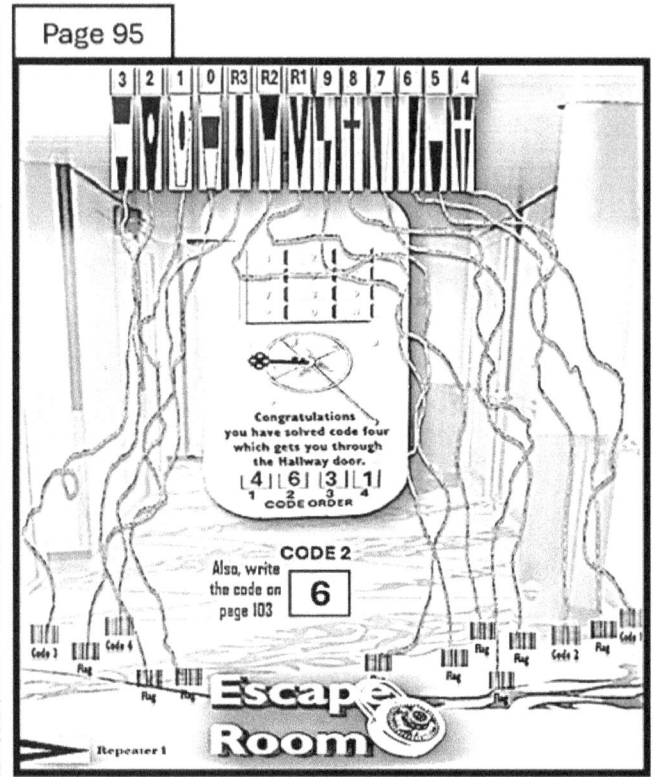

Page 99

Page 100
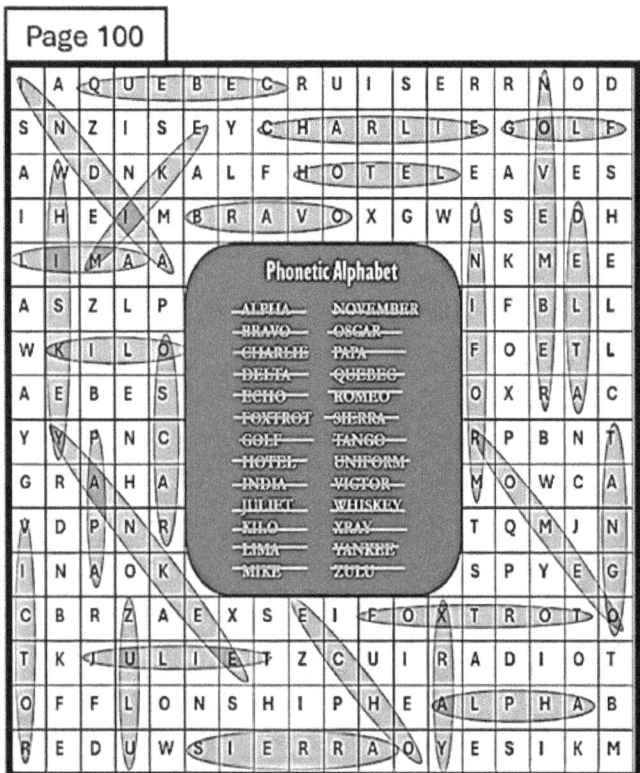

Page 102
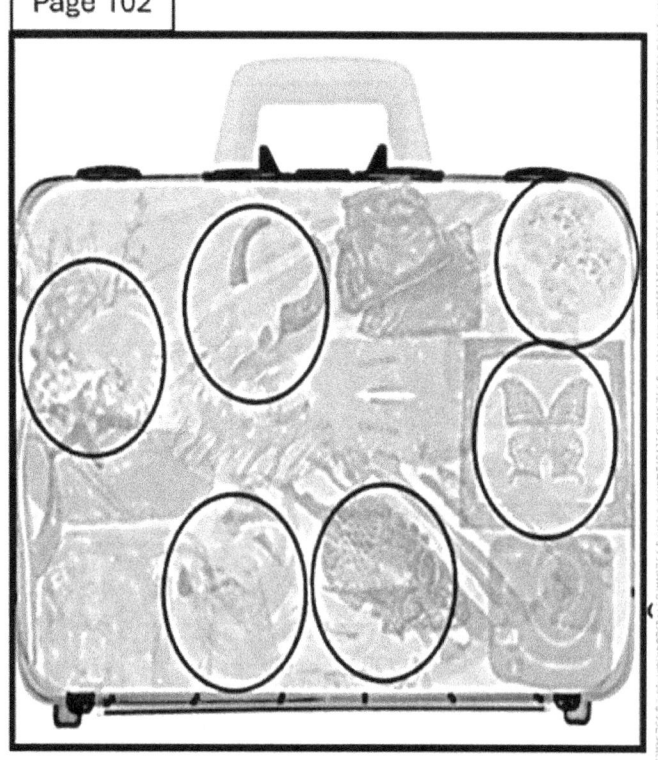

Answers Time

Page 103

Page 104

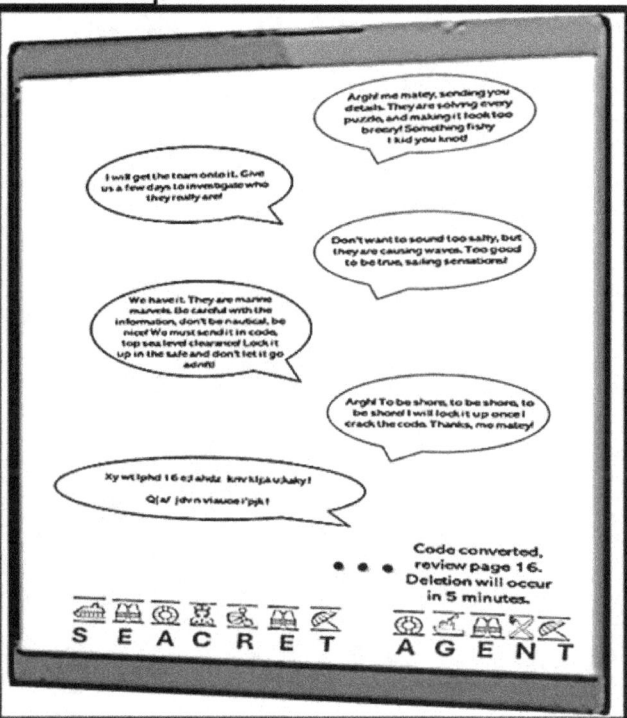

Page 105

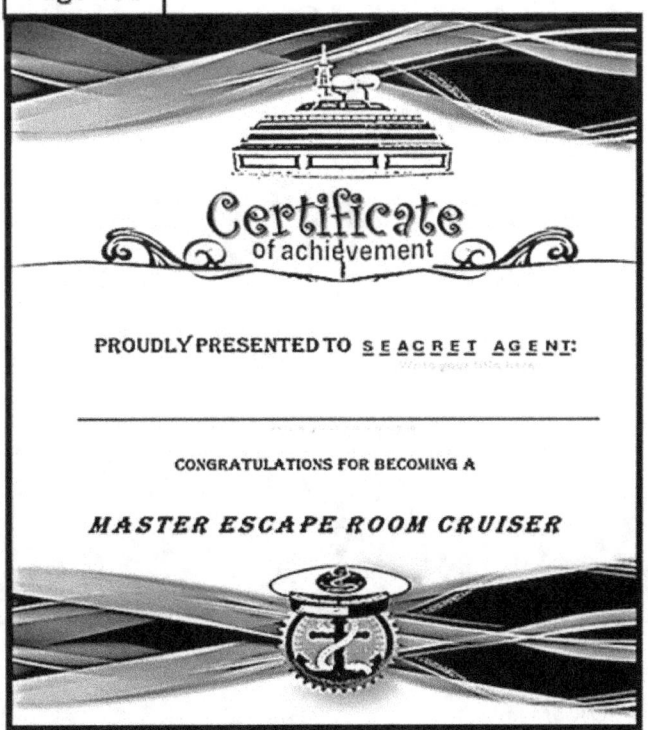

Farewell Time

Sea You later! Until we cruise again...

www.ingramcontent.com/pod-product-compliance
Lightning Source LLC
Chambersburg PA
CBHW081359070526
44583CB00020B/2600